War & Peace in the Middle East

MICHAEL SCOTT-BAUMANN

Contents

Chapter 1	Whose Land Is It Anyway?	2
Chapter 2	British Rule in Palestine	6
Chapter 3	Terrorism and the Birth of Israel	8
Chapter 4	The War of 1948–9	12
Chapter 5	The Suez War of 1956	14
Chapter 6	The Six-Day War of 1967	18
Chapter 7	The Yom Kippur War of 1973	24
Chapter 8	A People Without a Home – the Refugee Problem	28
Chapter 9	The Palestine Liberation Organisation	30
Chapter 10	War in Lebanon	34
Chapter 11	Peacemaking at the UN and Camp David	36
Chapter 12	The Role of the Superpowers (the United States and the USSR)	38
Chapter 13	The Intifada	40
Chapter 14	The Israeli–Palestinian Peace Agreement, 1993	42
Chapter 15	The Problems of Peacemaking	44
Chapter 16	Prospects for Peace	46
Glossary		47
Index		47
Acknowledgements		48

Hodder & Stoughton

A MEMBER OF THE HODDER HEADLINE GROUP

Whose Land Is It Anyway?

What are Jewish claims to the land based on? What is the basis of the Arab claim? Whose land is it anyway?

In 1948 the state of Israel was created out of the land of Palestine. Since then there has been almost continuous conflict between Israel and its Arab neighbours. The Middle East has hardly ever been out of the news. Why is this such a live issue? Whose land is it anyway?

A 'Cool it, quick!' An American newspaper's view of the Arab–Israeli conflict.

The Jewish claim to Palestine

From about 1500 BC, the Jewish people lived in the land of Palestine. In the time of Jesus – first century AD – Palestine was ruled by the Romans. In AD 70 and again in AD 135 the Jews rebelled against their Roman rulers. Roman soldiers crushed both revolts, destroyed the city of Jerusalem and expelled the Jews. Many thousands fled to neighbouring countries and over the next 200 years they settled in almost every part of the Roman empire (see source B). Many became merchants and farmers, bankers and craftsmen. Some became wealthy and even gained important positions in the governments of the new lands in which they lived.

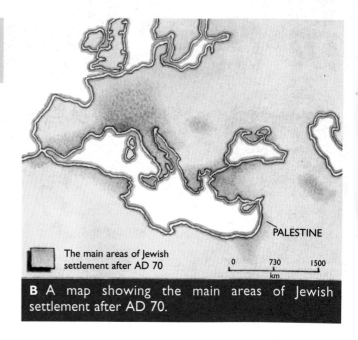

The main areas of Jewish settlement after AD 70

PALESTINE

0   730   1500
km

B A map showing the main areas of Jewish settlement after AD 70.

Then, in the Middle Ages, the Jews were expelled from western Europe and many settled in Russia and Poland. But they were often **persecuted**. Almost all Europeans were Christians and they often forced the Jews to live in separate areas. They were not allowed to vote or even to buy their own land. Such anti-Jewish behaviour is known as **anti-Semitism**.

In the nineteenth century, the country with the largest Jewish population was Russia. When the tsar, or emperor, was assassinated in 1881, there were many anti-Jewish riots. The new tsar's government encouraged the persecution of the Jews. **Synagogues** were burnt down, Jewish homes were attacked and thousands of Jews were killed. Many Russian Jews fled to western Europe and the US. But, even there, Jews found that they were not treated as equals and that they were sometimes suspected of being disloyal or untrustworthy.

'Next Year in Jerusalem'

For hundreds of years Jews dreamt and prayed that they would be able to celebrate 'Next Year in Jerusalem'. By the beginning of the twentieth century an increasing number of Jews were demanding a Jewish national home. By 1914, when the First World War broke out, these people were all agreed that this homeland would have to be in Palestine. This was the 'Promised Land', where the Jews (or Israelites) had lived some 2500 years before and where several thousands still remained.

C Making a home in the 'Promised Land'. A couple, recent immigrants from Europe, build a hut to live in.

Most Jews wanted to stay in the United States, France, Britain or Germany or wherever they were living, but a small number, especially from Russia, made their way to Palestine. They bought land there and started to farm and build homes. These people and all those who believed in a Jewish national homeland were called **Zionists** because Zion is the Jewish word for Jerusalem. Between 1880 and 1914, 60 000 Zionists settled in Palestine.

In 1917 the British were very keen to bring the United States into the First World War against Germany. The British believed that the Jews in America could influence their government's actions and so Britain declared its support for a Jewish homeland in Palestine. This declaration was made in the form of a letter to Lord Rothschild, a leading British Jew, in November 1917. It became known as the 'Balfour Declaration' because it was signed by the British Foreign Secretary, Lord Balfour.

D Adapted from the Balfour Declaration.

Foreign Office
December 2nd, 1917

Dear Lord Rothschild,

I have much pleasure in expressing to you, on behalf of His Majesty's Government, the following declaration of sympathy with Jewish Zionist ambitions. This has been approved by the Cabinet.

'His Majesty's Government view with favour the establishment in Palestine of a national home for the Jewish people. The Government will make every effort to help bring this about. It is clearly understood that nothing shall be done which may harm the civil and religious rights of existing non-Jewish communities in Palestine, or the rights and political status enjoyed by Jews in any other country.'

I should be grateful if you would bring this declaration to the knowledge of the Zionist Federation.

[Signed by Lord Balfour]

Zionist slogan about Palestine – 'a land without people for a people without land'.

1 What was the main aim of the Zionists?
2 Study source D carefully. For many years after this letter was published many Jews regarded the Balfour Declaration as a promise from the British government to help set up a Jewish state.
   a) Does it read like a promise?
   b) If so, a promise to do what?
   c) What does this document say about the non-Jews in Palestine? Why?

THE ARAB CLAIM TO PALESTINE

For many centuries the Arabs have lived in the lands which we call the Middle East. They form the majority of the population and all speak the same language, Arabic. In the seventh century AD most of the Arabs were converted to the religion of Islam. They became followers of Mohammed and are now known as Muslims. From their homeland in Arabia, they swept across the Middle East and North Africa in the seventh and eighth centuries spreading their new religion by force. Palestine was one of the countries they took over.

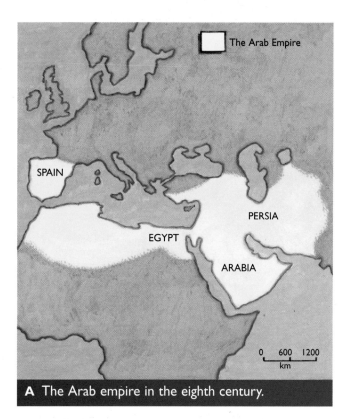

A The Arab empire in the eighth century.

In the Middle Ages, the Arab Muslims made important discoveries in mathematics and medicine. Their merchants bought and sold goods in Europe, Africa and Asia, and their lands grew rich. Then, in the sixteenth century, the Turks (who were also Muslims but not Arabs) conquered much of the Middle East. The Arabs were forced to pay taxes and provide soldiers for their Turkish masters.

In the late nineteenth century the Arabs tried several times to remove their Turkish rulers. Their aim was to re-establish Arab rule in the Middle East, including Palestine.

B In 1914 an Arab writer made this appeal:

> Arise, O ye Arabs! Take out the sword from the scabbard. Do not let an oppressive tyrant, who only despises you, remain in your country; cleanse your country from those who show their hatred to you, to your race and to your language.
>
> O ye Arabs! You all dwell in one land, you speak one language, so be also one nation and one land.
>
> Do not become divided amongst yourselves.

The Arabs and the First World War

The First World War was a turning point in the Arab struggle for independence as well as in the Jewish struggle for a homeland. Turkey fought on the German side against Britain and its allies. The British were afraid that their supplies of oil from Persia (or Iran, as it's known today) might be cut off by the Turks. So they decided to encourage the Arabs to rebel against their Turkish rulers and seek independence. The British High Commissioner in Egypt, Sir Herbert McMahon, exchanged several letters with Hussein, the Sharif of Mecca, an important Arab Muslim leader. McMahon promised that if the Arabs fought against the Turks, Britain would be 'prepared to recognise and support the independence of the Arabs'.

An Arab army was raised and led by Prince Faisal, the son of the Sharif of Mecca. The army blew up Turkish trains and disrupted the flow of military supplies to the Turkish soldiers. The Arabs felt that they had fought for their independence from the Turks and now deserved complete self-government.

Arab leaders were therefore angered when they heard that Britain and France had secretly agreed in 1916 to carve up Turkey's Arab lands after the war and share them out between themselves. (This agreement is known as the Sykes–Picot Agreement after the British and French politicians who made it.)

In 1919, the Peace of Versailles confirmed Arab fears. Britain and France were given **mandates**, or orders, to govern certain countries in the Middle East until the Arab people were considered ready to govern themselves. Britain was given mandates over Palestine and Iraq, and British troops and their administrators took control of these lands. France was granted mandates over Syria and Lebanon and soon sent troops in to take control.

C A Turkish water tower is blown up by Arab soldiers.

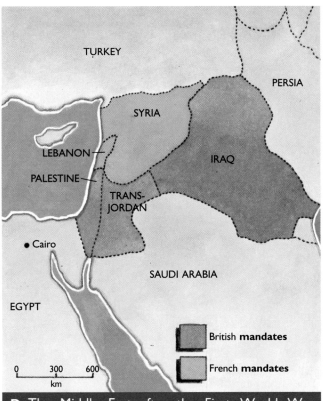

D The Middle East after the First World War showing the British and French mandates.

British **mandates**

French **mandates**

0   300   600
km

An Englishman, Major Lawrence, fought with the Arab army against the Turks. He later became known as 'Lawrence of Arabia'.

Q

1 Read source B.
 a) Who is the 'oppressive tyrant'?
 b) How does the writer think the Arabs should achieve their independence?
 c) What evidence is there to suggest that the writer does not wish to see several independent Arab nations emerge?
2 Why was the First World War a turning point in the struggle for Arab independence?
3 For what reasons do you think Britain and France might have made a secret deal in 1916 to divide Turkey's lands between them?
4 Britain made promises to the Jews, the Arabs and the French in the war. Which of these peoples would feel most betrayed after the war? Explain your answer.

British Rule in Palestine

Why did British rule lead to an Arab rebellion?

In 1917 British troops entered Jerusalem, the capital of Palestine, driving out the Turks. In 1919 Britain was given a mandate to govern Palestine. For the next 30 years the British government was to rule the country.

The Arabs of Palestine felt that they had simply exchanged Turkish rulers for British ones. Like the Arabs of Syria and Iraq, they were frustrated and disappointed that they had not been given their independence.

The Palestinian Arabs were even more angered by increasing Jewish **immigration** and the fact that Jews were buying land in 'their' country. The Jews only bought land in a few areas of Palestine, but in these areas the Arabs claimed they were being driven out. They also accused the British of being pro-Zionist.

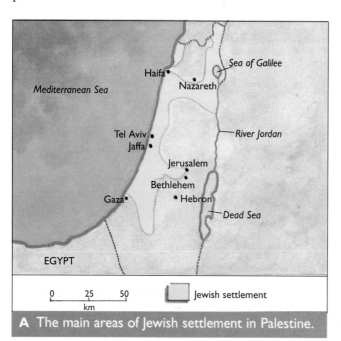

A The main areas of Jewish settlement in Palestine.

In 1921 an Arab mob set upon the Jews at the port of Jaffa and, after two days of rioting, 200 Jews and 120 Arabs were dead or wounded. In 1929 violence erupted again. This time it started in the city of Jerusalem, which is the Holy City for Jews but also the third most important city for Muslims. In August large Arab crowds attacked Jews inside and outside the city. The attacks spread throughout Palestine and, in four days, 133 Jews were killed

B The Dome of the Rock. Muslims believe that Mohammed rose to heaven from the Rock. Just below it is the Western or 'Wailing' Wall, which Jews believe to be the last remaining part of the ancient Jewish Temple.

(60 of these deaths were in the town of Hebron). During the attacks, 116 Arabs were also killed, mostly by the British police while trying to stop the anti-Jewish violence.

Similar outbreaks, though not so widespread, continued in the early 1930s, especially after 1933. In that year Adolf Hitler came to power in Germany and Nazi anti-Semitism drove many Jews abroad. Thousands fled to Palestine and by 1939 there were nearly 450 000 Jews in the country. Tension remained high and British government reports all came to the same conclusion – that the Arabs were afraid of losing their country as more and more of them became 'landless and discontented'.

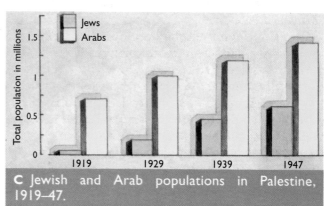

C Jewish and Arab populations in Palestine, 1919–47.

D Arab fighters, 1938.

The British were in an impossible position: if they allowed unrestricted immigration, Arab fears and violence would increase. But if they stopped or controlled immigration, the world would accuse them of inhumanity, of not caring for the Jews who were being persecuted by the Nazis.

Arab rebellion, 1936–9

In 1936, widespread fighting broke out as armed Arab bands attacked Jewish settlements. The British responded harshly. They hanged several Arab leaders and destroyed houses suspected of containing Arab terrorists or arms. They also helped to organise the Jewish Defence Force, the **Haganah** (which was set up in the 1920s and was later to develop into the Israeli army).

In 1937 the British government recommended the **partition** of Palestine into two separate states, one Jewish and a second Arab state. The Arabs rejected it and the fighting continued. With the help of more troops, better weapons and transport, the British forces gradually regained control of Palestine.

By 1939, when the rebellion ended, the British government had given up all further ideas of partition. It declared that Britain would continue to rule Palestine. It also said that it would restrict Jewish immigration (see source E). The British government adopted this policy because war was approaching and it feared the growth of friendship between Arab leaders and Germany. Britain needed to keep the friendship of the Arab countries so that oil supplies from the Middle East would continue to reach Britain.

The Jews were furious. Thousands took to the streets to demonstrate.

E In 1939 the British government declared:

For each of the next five years a limit of 10 000 Jewish immigrants will be allowed … apart from a special quota in the near future of 25 000 refugees as a contribution to the solution of the Jewish refugee problem.

After the period of five years no further Jewish immigration will be permitted unless the Arabs are prepared to agree to it.

1 Why were Palestinian Arabs angry about Jews immigrating to Palestine after the First World War?
2 In 1937 the British government recommended the partition of Palestine. Why was that idea dropped only two years later?
3 Look at source D.
  a) What impression does it give?
  b) This picture was found on the body of an Arab rebel leader who was killed by British troops. Why do you think he might have carried this photograph with him?
4 Using the sources and all you have learnt in this chapter, write 100–200 words to explain 'Why did the Arabs rebel in 1936?'

Terrorism and the Birth of Israel

Why did the British leave Palestine in 1948?
Why did Israel have such a bloody birth?

The King David Hotel in Jerusalem housed the British military headquarters in Palestine. It was protected by barbed wire, machine guns and patrolling soldiers. At noon on 22 July 1946, a lorry drove up to the entrance of the hotel kitchen. Men dressed as Arabs got out and unloaded their cargo of milk churns. They rolled them into the building. No one guessed that the milk churns contained high explosives or that the 'Arabs' were members of **Irgun**, a Jewish terrorist group. At 12.37 p.m. the explosion tore through the building killing 88 people, including 15 Jews.

Outrages like this were the result of hatred of British rule which developed amongst the Jews in Palestine. When they heard of the deaths of thousands of Jews in the Nazi **Holocaust**, Zionists began to demand that the Jews in Palestine should be granted their own independent state. They wanted a flag and an army of their own. They wanted a state where the survivors of Nazi persecution could live in peace.

During the Second World War, many Palestinian Jews fought in the British army but after the war they became impatient with British rule. Jewish leaders in Palestine thought the British were stopping them from having their own independent state. For this reason, Jewish terrorists began to bomb British army bases, barracks, bridges, trains and railways in Palestine. Between 1945 and 1948 over 300 British soldiers or officials were killed in Palestine.

Despite such acts there was widespread sympathy in Europe and the United States for the Jews who had survived the Nazi concentration camps. The large Jewish population in the United States gave millions of dollars to Zionist leaders and forced US President Truman to put pressure on the British.

A The King David Hotel was blown up by members of Irgun, a Jewish terrorist group in July 1946.

B This photograph appeared on the front page of the *Daily Express* in August 1947. It shows two British soldiers who had been hanged by members of Irgun. This hanging was in revenge for the execution of three of Irgun's members.

C The *Haganah* refugee ship arrived in Palestine with 25 000 illegal refugees on board. The banner on the ship reads, 'The Germans destroyed our families and homes – don't you destroy our hopes.'

'The choice for the Jews is between becoming a state and being exterminated,' (Chaim Weizmann, later President of Israel, writing to US President Truman, April 1948).

Truman said Britain should allow 100 000 Jewish refugees to enter Palestine. The British government refused, claiming that it would be unfair to the Arabs. British leaders said it would lead to civil war in Palestine.

The British continued to stop boatloads of illegal Jewish immigrants from landing in Palestine. In 1947, for example, a ship called *The Exodus*, carrying 4500 **refugees** from Europe, was prevented from landing its passengers and was sent back to Europe. As a result of actions like these, the British authorities came in for worldwide criticism.

The British were also exhausted after the war, with food shortages and rationing at home, and could hardly afford to keep 100 000 troops in Palestine. After 30 years of trying to solve the problems of Palestine, the British government announced, at the end of 1947, that it would hand over Palestine to the United Nations (UN).

Q

1 Why was the King David Hotel such an obvious target for Irgun to attack?
2 How did the Holocaust affect the situation in Palestine after the war?
3 Study source C. What does the banner say? How might this photograph have been used as **propaganda**?
4 Why do you think the British decided to hand over Palestine to the United Nations?
5 A Zionist leader, Israel Sieff, later wrote: 'The British government's policy towards Palestine had, by 1947, led to such bloody chaos that the British threw in their hand and asked for the future of Palestine to be dealt with by the United Nations.' To what extent do you agree with this interpretation?

THE UN PARTITION PLAN

In November 1947 the United Nations voted to divide Palestine and set up both a Jewish and an Arab state (see source A). The Palestinian Arabs rejected this plan, especially as the Jews were to be given the larger area. The Arabs did not wish to give up their land. They felt that the western powers should find a home for the Jews elsewhere. After all, the Arabs were not responsible for the Holocaust.

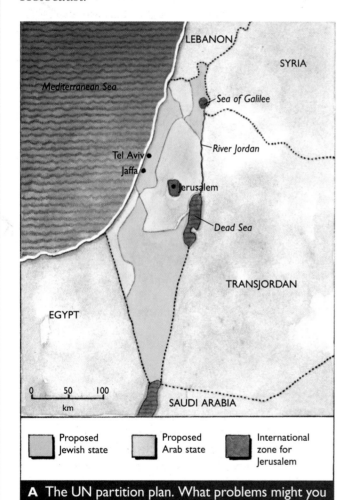

A The UN partition plan. What problems might you expect in a state which is divided into three parts?

Legend:
- Proposed Jewish state
- Proposed Arab state
- International zone for Jerusalem

Palestinian Jews accepted the plan but not all of them were happy with it. This was because many Jewish settlements were to be included in the Arab state and the Holy City of Jerusalem was to be an international zone.

B Menachem Begin, leader of Irgun, announced:

The partition of the homeland is illegal. It will never be recognised ... It will not bind the Jewish people. Jerusalem was and will for ever be our capital ...

MENAHEM BEIGIN

Age : 38 years
Height : 175 cms
Build : Thin
Complexion : Sallow
Hair : Dark
Eyes : Brown
Nose : Long, hooked
Peculiarities: Wears spectacles: flat footed; bad teeth
Nationality : Polish
Occupation : Clerk.

C WANTED! This is a photograph of Menachem Begin which was published by the British authorities in Palestine. A reward was offered for information leading to his arrest. Begin, who had lost both his parents and a brother in Nazi concentration camps, was the leader of Irgun. The Irgun was responsible for bombing the King David Hotel and the Deir Yassin massacre (see next page).

After the publication of the partition plan, fighting between Arabs and Jews grew worse. There was a particularly bitter struggle to control the roads leading to Jerusalem and massacres of civilians were carried out by both sides. Soldiers from Syria and Iraq began to cross into Palestine to help the Arabs, while the Haganah organised Jewish defence forces.

D Arab refugees flee from their homes.

By 14 May 1948, when the British finally withdrew, over 300 000 Arabs had fled from what was to become the new Jewish state. Arabs and Jews have argued about the causes of this flight ever since.

What caused the Arab flight?

In the weeks before the British withdrawal from Palestine, some of the bloodiest fighting took place in and around Jerusalem. In one incident, on 10 April 1948, Irgun fighters attacked the village of Deir Yassin (which was inside what was to be Arab territory under the UN partition plan) and killed the inhabitants.

E Menachem Begin wrote a book called *The Revolt* in 1951.

The civilian population of Deir Yassin was actually given a warning by us before the battle began. The fire of the enemy was murderous. Our men were compelled to fight for every house: to overcome the enemy they used large numbers of hand-grenades.

Throughout the Arab world and the world at large, a wave of lying propaganda was let loose about 'Jewish atrocities' … the Arabs began to flee in terror, even before they clashed with Jewish forces … This Arab propaganda spread a legend of terror amongst Arabs and Arab troops, who were seized with panic at the mention of Irgun soldiers. The legend was worth half a dozen battalions to the forces of Israel.

F A French Red Cross official, who visited the scene of the massacre the next day, wrote a report.

The press and radio spread the news everywhere among Arabs as well as Jews. In this way a general terror was built up among the Arabs … Driven by fear, the Arabs left their homes to find shelter among their kindred [relatives]; first isolated farms, then villages, and in the end, whole towns were evacuated.

G The Britain/Israel Public Affairs Centre, an Israeli information service, takes a different view:

If the Arabs were so attached to their land, why did they leave it during a crisis? The blame must belong to Arab leaders who, expecting a quick victory by their combined armies over Israel, encouraged Arabs to leave Palestine, promising that on their return they would be able to claim the property of the Jews as well. Arab propaganda led them to fear what would happen to them if they stayed, and threatened that they would also be considered traitors to the Arab cause.

H S. Penrose, a British historian, wrote:

There is no doubt that frightful massacres such as that which took place at Deir Yassin in April 1948 were carried out for the major purpose of frightening the Arab population and causing them to take flight. The Zionist radio repeated incessantly for the benefit of Arab listeners 'Remember Deir Yassin!'.

I Erskine Childers, an Irish journalist, wrote in 1961:

I next decided to test the charge that the Arab evacuation orders were broadcast by Arab radio – which could be done thoroughly because the BBC monitored all Middle East broadcasts throughout 1948. The records, and companion ones by a US monitoring unit, can be seen at the British Museum.

There was not a single order, or appeal, or suggestion about evacuation from Palestine from any Arab radio station, inside or outside Palestine in 1948. There is a repeated monitored record of Arab appeal, even flat orders, to the civilians of Palestine to stay put.

1 Why do you think the bloodiest fighting took place around Jerusalem?
2 a) Who does Begin (source E) blame for the Arab flight?
   b) What do you think he means by ' The legend was worth half a dozen battalions to the forces of Israel'?
   c) What is there in the **provenance** of this source which might lead you to question its reliability?
3 Read source G. Who is blamed for the Arab flight? How does the author explain this?
4 a) What does the author of source H see as the motive for the attack on Deir Yassin?
   b) Does the last sentence prove that Irgun attacked Deir Yassin in order to cause the Arabs to flee from their homes?
5 a) Which of the earlier sources, if any, does source I contradict?
   b) How useful is this source for a historian studying the causes of the Arab flight?
6 'Sources E and F are first-hand accounts and therefore more reliable as evidence for the historian studying the causes of the Arab flight than the other sources.' Explain whether you agree with this statement, making reference to each of the sources.

The War of 1948–9

How did Israel survive its first war?

When the state of Israel was created, none of the Arab states recognised its right to exist. As far as they were concerned, Palestine had been occupied by Zionists and Israel ought to be destroyed. Over the next 25 years there were to be four major wars between Israel and its Arab neighbours.

The next four chapters examine the causes and consequences of each of those wars. They look at the underlying or general causes as well as at particular or immediate causes. They also explain why much bigger Arab states have been unable to defeat the Israelis on the battlefield.

The invasion of Israel

On 14 May 1948, David Ben-Gurion announced the founding of the new state of Israel. Immediately, armies from the Arab states of Egypt, Syria, Transjordan, Lebanon and Iraq invaded.

The Arabs of Palestine were disorganised and lacked good leaders. Many of the armies from the other Arab states were poorly trained or badly equipped. They certainly had no coordinated plan of campaign. The only efficient and experienced Arab force was the Arab Legion from Transjordan. It captured and held the eastern part, the Old City, of Jerusalem.

On the other fronts, the Israelis resisted and the United Nations ordered a cease-fire in June. The Israelis now reorganised and acquired fresh weapons. Fighting broke out twice more and by January 1949 Israel had driven out the Arab armies and even occupied some of the land which the UN had granted to the Arabs (see source C). In addition about 700 000 Palestinian Arabs had fled their homes. Israel refused to hand back the land it had occupied in the fighting, while the Arab governments refused to accept that the state of Israel existed. There was no peace treaty, only a truce.

A Palestinian Arab troops, 1948.

B Israeli Jewish troops, 1948.

How did Israel survive?

The Israeli state had survived its first great test because the Jews had defended it fiercely and successfully in the war. Jewish soldiers were disciplined and hardened by their experience in fighting with the British in the Second World War and against them after it. They were well-led and organised. Above all, they were fighting to save their new country.

The people of Israel realised that they were surrounded by enemies. They were convinced that the Arabs wished to drive them into the sea and would try to attack again. The Israeli army would have to be constantly on the alert. Israeli men were liable to be called up for military service.

The Israeli army helped to shape the new nation as well as defend it. The Jews of Israel had come from different parts of Europe and the US. Between 1949 and 1954 another 700 000 arrived. Many were from North Africa and other parts of the Middle East. In the army they all received a similar training, lived together and had to learn Hebrew. It was experience in the army that helped to make the newly arrived Jews into true Israelis.

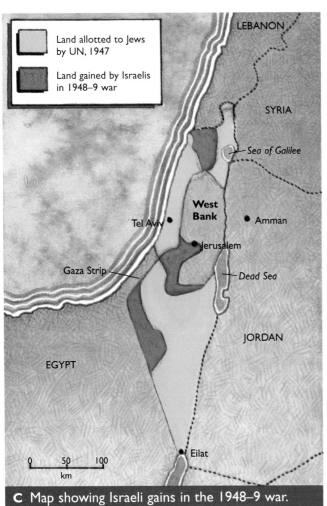

C Map showing Israeli gains in the 1948–9 war.

Key:
- Land allotted to Jews by UN, 1947
- Land gained by Israelis in 1948–9 war

Places shown: LEBANON, SYRIA, Sea of Galilee, West Bank, Tel Aviv, Amman, Jerusalem, Gaza Strip, Dead Sea, JORDAN, EGYPT, Eilat. Scale: 0 50 100 km

Many Israelis went to live and work on kibbutzim. These were (and still are) large cooperative farms in which all the property and work was shared. Different families ate together and shared living quarters.

With financial aid from the United States and Germany, the Israelis irrigated and cultivated vast areas of desert. They established chemical, shipbuilding and motor industries.

A nation on guard

Israel is a small country and none of the Israelis felt really safe from attack. They feared that the Palestinian Arabs, most of whom had left Israel, would try to win back the lands they had lost. Nearly half a million Arabs had fled to the two areas of Palestine that were not taken over by Israel. These two areas were the West Bank, which became part of the state of Jordan, and Gaza, a thin strip of land which the Egyptians controlled (see source C). Palestinian fighters, or **fedayeen**, on the West Bank and in Gaza carried out raids into Israeli territory. The Israelis retaliated fiercely.

Q

1 Look at sources A and B. How do they compare? In what ways are these photographs useful for an understanding of the outcome of the 1948–9 war?

2 a) Draw a table like the one below. Then, using the text and sources in this chapter, make notes in order to complete it.

Reasons for Israel's victory, 1948–9	
Israeli strengths	Arab weaknesses

b) What other factors, besides those mentioned in this chapter, might help to explain Israeli success?

c) Now write 100–200 words in answer to the question 'How do you explain Israel's success in the war of 1948–9?'

The Suez War of 1956

What led to the outbreak of a second Arab–Israeli war? Why did Britain and France become so involved? Who won and who lost the war?

The Arab states were shocked by their defeat at the hands of the Israelis in 1948–9. It showed how weak and divided they were. It made them bitterly anti-western. The Arabs felt that the United States had bullied the United Nations into creating the new state of Israel. They suspected that the western powers would use Israel as a base from which to keep an eye on the new Arab states.

Also, the Arab governments were still not completely independent, even after the Second World War. The mandates had ended but there were still many western troops and advisers in the Middle East. For instance, in Egypt, which was the most powerful Arab state, there were 70 000 British troops in the Suez Canal area. The Canal was owned and run by the British and French. It was a vital route for oil supplies to the West.

A group of young Egyptian army officers was determined to get rid of the British troops and achieve full independence for their country. In 1952, after years of planning, they overthrew the unpopular monarchy and took control of the government. Their leader was General Neguib, but the real organiser was Colonel Nasser.

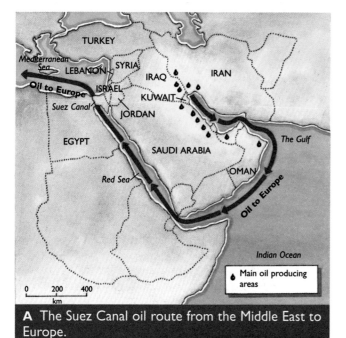

A The Suez Canal oil route from the Middle East to Europe.

B Colonel Nasser was one of the army officers who overthrew the unpopular Egyptian King and his government in 1952. In 1954 he became President of Egypt.

Nasser

In 1954 Nasser became President and, after long discussions, he persuaded the British to withdraw their troops from the Suez Canal zone. Britain and the United States still wished to keep on good terms with Nasser. They wanted Arab support in the Middle East against communist Russia. They particularly wanted an alliance with Egypt as it was the strongest, most developed Arab nation, and because the Suez Canal passed through its territory.

Nasser wanted Egypt to be neutral and was not willing to join an anti-Russian alliance. He did, however, need arms to strengthen Egypt's army. This became very urgent in February 1955 when the Israeli government decided to hit back at Egypt for encouraging Palestinian raids into Israel. Israeli troops attacked the Egyptian army headquarters in Gaza and killed 50 Egyptian soldiers. For three days Palestinian refugees in Gaza ran riot and demanded: 'Arms, give us arms, we shall defend ourselves!' Even in Cairo, the crowds wanted revenge.

The Suez Crisis, 1956

In September 1955, Nasser shocked the West by agreeing to buy Russian arms from Czechoslovakia.

Britain and the United States thought they could still control Nasser because he depended on them for money to build the Aswan High Dam. This was a huge project on the River Nile which would create hydro-electric power for Egyptian industry and allow vast areas of land to be irrigated. In July 1956, Britain and the USA refused to lend Egypt any more money. Perhaps they hoped to persuade Nasser to be more cooperative. Maybe they thought they could force the Egyptians to replace

> **Nasser told the crowd:**
> 'We dug the Canal with our lives, our skulls, our bones, our blood.'

him. But Nasser shocked the West again. He was not going to be pushed around any longer. He would prove that Egypt was independent now. Before a huge crowd, on 26 July, he announced that the Suez Canal was 'our Canal'. Egypt would **nationalise** it and use the profits to build the Aswan Dam. He said that Britain and France could 'choke on their rage'. This daring act thrilled the Arabs in Egypt and elsewhere.

Britain and France were furious. The British Prime Minister, Anthony Eden, was determined not to let Nasser 'have his thumb on our windpipe'. The British and French withdrew their pilots who guided ships through the Canal. But the Egyptians kept it running and the traffic increased.

C In September 1956, Eden wrote to the US President:

> … the seizure of the Suez Canal is, we are convinced, the opening move in a planned campaign designed by Nasser to expel all western influence and interests from Arab countries. He believes that if he can get away with this, his prestige in Arabia will be so great that [Arab] governments will have to place their united oil resources under the control of a united Arabia led by Egypt and under Russian influence. When that moment comes Nasser can deny oil to western Europe and we here shall all be at his mercy.

On 24 October the British and French Foreign Ministers secretly met the Israeli Prime Minister, David Ben-Gurion, in France. Ben-Gurion wished to teach the Egyptians a lesson. He wanted to end the border raids from Gaza and force Egypt to recognise the state of Israel. He also wanted to break the Egyptian **blockade** of the Tiran Straits which prevented ships from reaching the port of Eilat (see source C on page 13). Furthermore, he was worried about the increasing military strength of Egypt and the fact that the armies of Egypt, Syria and Jordan had been put under the same command.

France, like Britain and Israel, also wanted to teach Egypt, especially Nasser, a lesson. Nasser had been sending aid to the Algerians in their fight against French rule.

There were other high-level meetings between Britain, France and Israel. Although it was denied at the time, a joint campaign against Egypt was being planned.

D This cartoon was published in Britain after Nasser nationalised the Suez Canal.

1 Draw a table like the one below in order to summarise the main events leading up to the outbreak of the 1956 war. In the case of each event, add a sentence or some notes to explain the motive of those involved. The first one has been done for you.

Sept 1955	Nasser decided to buy Russian arms	He needed arms for defence against Israel and the West would not supply them
July 1956		
26 July		
24 Oct		

2 Study source C again.
 a) What are Eden's main fears?
 b) How do you think Nasser would answer each of these accusations?
 c) To whom was Eden writing? How might this influence the content and style of his letter?
3 What is the message of the cartoon in source D? How useful is it as a historical source?

THE FIGHTING OVER SUEZ, 1956

On 29 October Israeli forces invaded the Sinai peninsula in Egypt and advanced towards the Suez Canal. The following day, Britain and France ordered Egypt and Israel to cease fighting and withdraw 16 kilometres from the Canal. If either side refused, Britain and France would use force. The Israelis were a long way from the Canal and therefore agreed, but Nasser refused to withdraw from the Canal because it was Egyptian territory.

On 31 October, British and French planes bombed Egyptian airfields and destroyed most of the air force. On 5 November British and French troops landed at Port Said and advanced along the Canal. Egypt responded by sinking ships to block the Canal.

At the United Nations, the Arab states condemned the Anglo-French action. They stopped oil supplies to the West. Even more worrying for Britain was the fact that its ally, the United States, condemned the action. The US government was furious that Britain and France had used force. It threatened to cut off financial aid to Britain, which would ruin the economy. The Russians went further and threatened to use military force. On 6 November, the UN proclaimed a cease-fire and sent an emergency force to the Canal. The British and French withdrew.

Leader of the Arab world

Nasser became the hero of the whole Arab world. He had stood up to Britain and France, who had dominated the Middle East for so long, and he had gained complete control of the Canal. He lost territory when the Israelis captured Sinai, but they were persuaded to withdraw by the Americans in 1957. In addition, Nasser could claim that the Egyptian army had only been defeated because the Israelis had Anglo-French support.

A Port Said, at the northern end of the Suez Canal, was bombed by the British navy before troops landed.

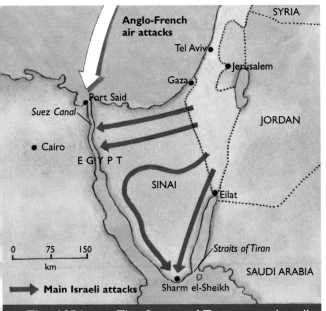

B The 1956 war. The Straits of Tiran were Israel's outlet to trade with Asia and Africa.

The Israelis also made gains. When they withdrew from Sinai, UN troops moved in to guard the border between Egypt and Israel. In particular, UN forces were posted to Gaza to prevent more raids on Israel and to Sharm-el-Sheikh to guard the passage of Israeli shipping through the Straits of Tiran.

One of the main effects of the Suez crisis was to make many of the Arab states even more anti-western and willing to seek Russian aid. The Soviet Union now began to supply most of Egypt's weapons and to pay for the building of the Aswan Dam and many other projects. However, Nasser did not want Egypt to be tied to Russia and he was certainly not a communist. He wanted Egypt and the other Arab states to be neutral.

In 1964 Nasser invited the leaders of the Arab states to a conference in Cairo. Although many of them mistrusted each other, one thing united them all: opposition to the state of Israel and support for the Palestinians.

Who won and who lost the Suez–Sinai War?

C An American historian writing in 1979:

> Curiously, in western eyes, the Suez War made Nasser a hero. One of its purposes was to destroy him and at the beginning of the fighting few would have given him even odds to survive. However, he did; more, he claimed with some justice a political victory within a military defeat.

When the British and French forces landed on the Suez Canal, Nasser ordered the sinking of ships which were filled with concrete in order to obstruct the British and French advance along the Canal.

D Moshe Dayan, an Israeli army general, writing in his memoirs, *The Story of My Life*:

> It may be said right away that the three main purposes were achieved: our ships could now use the Gulf of Aqaba; an end to fedayeen terrorism; and the prevention of a joint attack on Israel by the Egypt–Syria–Jordan military command. In addition the victory in Sinai meant that Israel emerged as a state that would be welcomed as a friend and ally. Further, Nasser learned to respect the power of Israel's army.

E Nasser sums up the results:

> We were able after Suez to take over all the foreign property in our country and therefore the Suez War regained the wealth of the Egyptian people to be used in the interests of the Egyptian people. Then, of course, it was clear for the Egyptian people that they could defend their country and secure the independence of their country.

1 Study source A. How might the Egyptian government have used a photograph like this?
2 a) 'The Israelis gained little from the war because they had to withdraw from the land they had conquered.' Does source D and what you have read in this chapter support this view?
   b) In what ways had Nasser won 'a political victory within a military defeat' (source C)?

Extended writing
Using the sources and the text of this chapter, write 250–400 words to answer the question: 'Who gained more from the 1956 war – Israel or Egypt?' Explain your verdict fully. You may find it helpful to mention the following:
a) Who gained in military terms?
b) Who gained politically?
c) Who became stronger or became more secure?

6

The Six-Day War of 1967

Who was to blame for the war? How did the Israelis achieve such a devastating victory? What did Israel gain from the war?

The Palestine Liberation Organisation

At their meeting in Cairo in 1964, leaders of the Arab states decided to set up the Palestine Liberation Organisation (**PLO**). The aim of this organisation was to win back the land which the Palestinians had lost in 1948–9. In 1965 a **guerrilla** group called **Fatah**, which was part of the PLO, carried out its first raid on Israel. This group carried out many armed raids into Israel over the next few years. It also planted bombs in Israeli government buildings and mined roads.

The state of Israel had become richer and more modern since the 1956 war. Industries had been built and huge areas of desert irrigated. Israel had also spent vast sums of money on its armed forces to defend itself. This was possible only with huge gifts from abroad. Most of this aid came from the United States. In fact, the US government and American Jews sent about $1000 million a year to Israel. The US government felt that Israel was a close, firm friend in a troubled part of the world and it knew that Russia was arming Egypt and Syria.

Fatah had its bases in three countries: Syria, Jordan and Lebanon. All three bordered Israel. Israeli villages were often attacked by Fatah guerrillas. The governments of Lebanon and Jordan tried to restrict PLO activities because they were afraid of Israeli **reprisals**. The Syrians, however, were very keen to support the PLO. They encouraged Fatah's raids against Israel and supplied men and arms. The only neighbouring state from which Israel was not attacked was Egypt. This was because United Nations troops had been placed on the border between Egypt and Israel after the 1956 war to prevent further clashes.

In 1966 the Syrians became even more anti-Israel and accused the Egyptian government of not supporting them. They taunted Nasser, saying that he was hiding behind the protection of the UN troops. Nasser was deeply hurt. He wanted his country to remain peaceful, but he also wanted to remain the leader of the Arab world. So, in November 1966, he signed a defence agreement

A A young Fatah member being trained in the use of his weapon. Raids by Fatah and Israeli reprisals contributed to the tension leading to war in 1967.

with the Syrian government, although he hoped to avoid starting another war with Israel.

Tension was not only high in Syria, for a week later a mine exploded on the Israel–Jordan frontier, killing three Israeli soldiers. The Israelis retaliated by attacking the nearest Jordanian village. In early 1967 there were many more raids and reprisals across the borders. Israeli villages near the Syrian border were frequently shelled by Syrian guns. In April 1967 the Israeli air force shot down six Syrian fighter planes after a Syrian attack on northern Israel. In May, Russia warned its Syrian ally that Israel was preparing to attack.

The crisis of May 1967

On 18 May Nasser asked the UN commander to remove his troops from Egyptian soil. He wanted to prove that Egypt was completely independent. The UN forces could stay on Egyptian territory only as long as Egypt allowed them. The UN Secretary-General proposed that the UN troops be placed on the Israeli side of the border. The Israelis refused so the UN troops were withdrawn.

The PLO and the leaders of Syria, Jordan and Iraq now challenged Nasser to take control of the Gulf of Aqaba again. On 22 May Egypt closed the

B A cartoon published in an Arab newspaper in May 1967. Each cannon has the name of a different Arab state on it.

Gulf of Aqaba to Israeli shipping. The Israelis regarded this as 'an act of aggression' against Israel, and claimed that the United States, France and Britain had 'guaranteed' free passage for all shipping through the Gulf of Aqaba in 1957.

Meanwhile, a war fever was being whipped up in the press and radio in several Arab states.

C On 24 May the Syrian Defence Minister taunted the Israelis:

> We shall never call for, nor accept peace. We have resolved to drench this land with your blood and throw you into the sea for good.

D On 29 May Nasser spoke to the Egyptian parliament:

> Preparations have already been made. We are now ready to confront Israel. The issue now at hand is not the Gulf of Aqaba, the Straits of Tiran, or the withdrawal of the UN forces, but the rights of the Palestine people. It is the aggression which took place in Palestine in 1948 with the collaboration of Britain and the United States.

Nasser demanded that Israel should allow the Palestinian refugees to return to Israel and that Israel should give up the land taken in the 1948–9 war (which was more than the UN had offered it). Maybe he thought that Israel would give way and he could win a victory without a war.

In Jordan, King Hussein wanted to avoid war and remain neutral if fighting broke out. But half the population of Jordan was Palestinian, and newspapers and demonstrations demanded

revenge for 1948. On 30 May King Hussein signed a defence treaty with Egypt.

War broke out a week later.

1 Read sources C and D again. 'These speeches, by political leaders, were made for propaganda purposes. This therefore makes them unreliable as evidence for the causes of the war.' Do you agree?

2 a) Make a table like the one below in order to summarise the events leading up to the outbreak of war.

Date	Event	Effect/Result
18 May		
22 May		
24 May		
29 May		
30 May		

b) These events, and the fears and insecurity they caused, were the immediate causes of the Six-Day War. What were the longer-term, or more general, causes?

c) Now write 200–300 words to answer the question 'Who was to blame for the Six-Day War of 1967?'

THE FIGHTING, JUNE 1967

The Israelis feared a repeat of 1948. They were surrounded by warlike Arab states. They decided to attack first. Just after dawn on Monday 5 June the Israeli air force took off. It attacked the Arab planes on the ground. Within four hours it had destroyed the air forces of Egypt, Syria and Jordan. The war was to last six days but the Israelis had virtually won on the first day. They had complete control of the skies. The main facts of the fighting are presented in the table below.

> In less than three hours, on the morning of 5 June, over 300 Egyptian planes were destroyed.

A Israeli crews scramble to man their tanks.

Date	Israel v. Egypt	Israel v. Jordan	Israel v. Syria
Monday 5 June	Israeli planes bombed all 19 Egyptian airfields and wrecked 300 planes. Israeli troops advanced into the Gaza Strip and Sinai desert.	The Israelis destroyed the Jordanian air force. Jordanian troops attacked West Jerusalem.	Israeli planes crippled the Syrian air force.
Tuesday 6 June	The Israelis raced the Egyptian forces to the Suez Canal. The Israeli air force destroyed many Egyptian tanks and other vehicles, while Israeli ground forces destroyed or captured the rest.	Heavy fighting for control of Jerusalem and the West Bank of the River Jordan.	
Wednesday 7 June	The Israelis won complete control of Sinai and accepted the UN call for a cease-fire with Egypt.	The Israelis captured all of Jerusalem. Jordan accepted the UN demand for a cease-fire.	
Thursday 8 June	Egypt accepted the cease-fire call.	Israel won complete control of all the West Bank of the River Jordan.	
Friday 9 June			Israeli troops attacked the Golan Heights.
Saturday 10 June			Israelis seized the Golan Heights. Syria accepted the UN call for a cease-fire.

Israelis triumphant

The Israelis had won a brilliant military victory. The Arabs had lost 15 000 men while the Israelis had lost less than a thousand. The Arabs had larger armies but their air forces were destroyed. The Arabs had modern Soviet missiles and other weapons but the Israelis had the most advanced US electronic equipment and were highly skilled and well trained. Above all, the Israelis believed they were fighting for their nation's survival.

B Moshe Dayan, Israeli Defence Minister. Dayan had been imprisoned by the British in 1939. He was later released and fought in the British army in Syria where he lost an eye. In 1956 he organised the Israeli campaign in Sinai and in 1967 he became the hero of the Six-Day War.

The Arabs in defeat

The Arabs felt more hostile than ever. They blamed their defeat on the United States, Britain and other European powers, whom they accused of helping Israel in the war.

C In August 1967, Arab leaders declared their main principles:

No peace with Israel, no recognition of Israel, no negotiation with it. We insist on the rights of the Palestinian people in their country.

The three main oil-producing Arab states of Saudi Arabia, Kuwait and Libya agreed to pay £135 million annually to Egypt and Jordan, the two states which had suffered most in the war. The Soviet Union decided to replace the weapons which its allies, Egypt and Syria, had lost.

> Far from strangling the state of Israel at birth, the Arab wars gave Israel the opportunity to expand its borders.

D In November 1967 the United Nations passed Resolution 242. This called for:

a) **The withdrawal of Israeli armed forces from the territories occupied in the recent conflict.**

b) **Respect for the right of every state in the area to live in peace within secure and recognised boundaries, free from threats or acts of force.**

However, the Israelis would not withdraw and the Arabs still refused to recognise the state of Israel.

E Victorious Israeli soldiers at the Western Wall in Jerusalem. The Wall is the one remaining part of the ancient Jewish Temple which was destroyed by the Romans.

1 How do you explain why, yet again, the Israelis defeated their Arab enemies?

2 The Arab states of Egypt, Syria and Jordan suffered heavy losses in the war. Who helped them to recover afterwards?

3 Why did the Six-Day War make another war more likely?

WINNING THE PEACE

The Israelis won a stunning military victory in June 1967. Now they had to win the peace. They had to decide what to do with the lands they had conquered. In Chapter 9 you will examine the effects of the war from a Palestinian point of view. In this chapter you will examine the Israeli viewpoint.

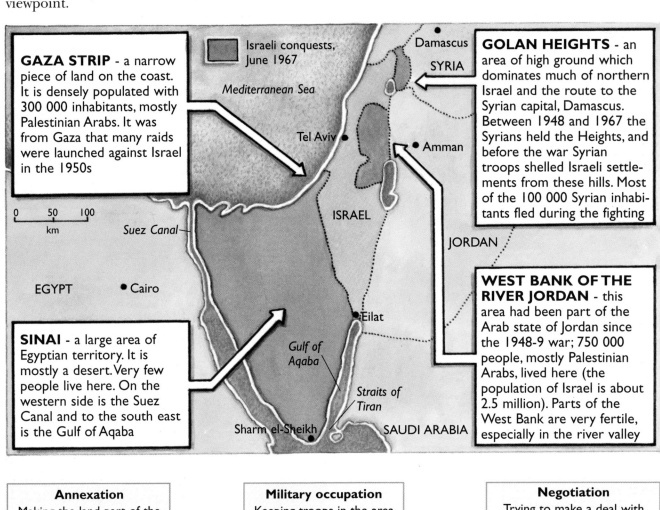

GAZA STRIP - a narrow piece of land on the coast. It is densely populated with 300 000 inhabitants, mostly Palestinian Arabs. It was from Gaza that many raids were launched against Israel in the 1950s

Israeli conquests, June 1967

Mediterranean Sea

Tel Aviv

Damascus

SYRIA

GOLAN HEIGHTS - an area of high ground which dominates much of northern Israel and the route to the Syrian capital, Damascus. Between 1948 and 1967 the Syrians held the Heights, and before the war Syrian troops shelled Israeli settlements from these hills. Most of the 100 000 Syrian inhabitants fled during the fighting

Amman

ISRAEL

JORDAN

Suez Canal

EGYPT   • Cairo

SINAI - a large area of Egyptian territory. It is mostly a desert. Very few people live here. On the western side is the Suez Canal and to the south east is the Gulf of Aqaba

Eilat

Gulf of Aqaba

Straits of Tiran

Sharm el-Sheikh

SAUDI ARABIA

WEST BANK OF THE RIVER JORDAN - this area had been part of the Arab state of Jordan since the 1948-9 war; 750 000 people, mostly Palestinian Arabs, lived here (the population of Israel is about 2.5 million). Parts of the West Bank are very fertile, especially in the river valley

0 50 100
km

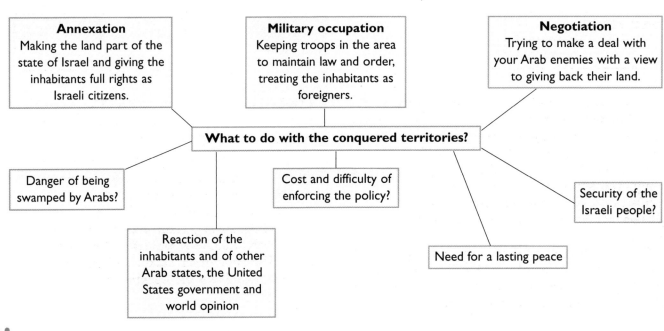

Annexation
Making the land part of the state of Israel and giving the inhabitants full rights as Israeli citizens.

Military occupation
Keeping troops in the area to maintain law and order, treating the inhabitants as foreigners.

Negotiation
Trying to make a deal with your Arab enemies with a view to giving back their land.

What to do with the conquered territories?

Danger of being swamped by Arabs?

Cost and difficulty of enforcing the policy?

Security of the Israeli people?

Reaction of the inhabitants and of other Arab states, the United States government and world opinion

Need for a lasting peace

Conquered lands	Policy options		
	Annexation	Military occupation	Negotiation
Sinai			Negotiate with Egypt as it's a large, barren area and, therefore, not worth keeping. But we do need security so we should offer it back in return for a peace treaty and the promise of free shipping in Gulf of Aqaba. If they don't agree, we keep it under military occupation.
Gaza			
West Bank			
Golan Heights			

The Israelis argued with each other about the
occupied territories (and they still do today, as you
will see later) but most of them agreed that Jews
must dominate them. In fact, the Israeli
government decided on military occupation of the
conquered lands. It also ordered the army to
confiscate Arab land and to build Jewish
settlements in order to make the areas more
secure.

On one point, in particular, the Israelis were
united. They had taken control of East Jerusalem,
the Old City, for the first time in nearly 2000 years.
They were determined to hold on to it.

Israel's borders were now secure. There was a
buffer zone, or cushion, between its land and each
of its three main enemies:

- *Syria.* Villages in the north of Israel were safe
  from Syrian artillery now that the Israelis
  controlled the Golan Heights.
- *Jordan.* Military fortifications were built on the
  banks of the River Jordan while the land on the
  West Bank of the river was controlled by Israel.
- *Egypt.* The Sinai desert formed a huge buffer
  between Israel and the Egyptian army.

7

The Yom Kippur War of 1973

Why did Egypt and Syria attack Israel in 1973? Was this the Arabs' first 'victory' over Israel?

The Arabs are a proud people, yet they had been humiliated in the Six-Day War. They longed to regain their honour and their pride. Only by defeating Israel could they do this.

At the end of the Six-Day War, there was no peace treaty. In fact, fighting broke out again between Israel and Egypt in 1968. The Egyptians wished to clear the Suez Canal of sunken ships. The Israelis would only agree to this if their ships were allowed through the Canal. Over the next two years there were many clashes across the Canal. Both Egypt and Israel lost many men and weapons. By 1970 both sides were tiring. Nasser had not received the support he had hoped for from other Arab states. He appeared willing to recognise Israel. Then, in September 1970, he died. He had played an important part in world affairs for nearly 20 years.

Anwar Sadat took over as President of Egypt. Like Nasser, he was an army officer. He promised his people that the year 1971 'would *not* end without the conflict with Israel having been settled'.

There was still great tension on the Suez Canal. Neither side could use the Canal although both sides wanted to, and it seemed that fighting could flare up at any time. Egypt had to keep nearly one million men ready to fight and this was very expensive. It needed peace in order to clear the Canal and rebuild its cities. But Egypt also wanted to win back Sinai, the land east of the Suez Canal which it had lost in 1967.

No peace, no war

Sadat was prepared to recognise the state of Israel in order to regain the lost land. However, the Israelis were unwilling to discuss it and Sadat knew he could not defeat Israel in war. He therefore tried to get help from the United States to force Israel to give way. The United States was very friendly with Israel, but Sadat knew the US government wanted peace and friendship with the Arab states in the Middle East. As an Arab, Sadat hoped he could persuade the US government to use its influence with the Israelis. He sacked the members of his government who were anti-American. The United States, however, was too busy with the war in Vietnam. Besides, the six million Jews in America would oppose any attempt by the US government to 'bully' the Israelis. So the year 1971 ended, as it had begun, with 'no peace, no war'.

Egypt and Syria prepare for war

Sadat then tried to obtain support from the Russians but, in return for supplying arms to Egypt, they wanted more control in Egyptian affairs. The Egyptian government could not stand any more Russian interference and so, in 1972, Sadat expelled all 15 000 Russian advisers who had been training Egypt's armed forces. This still made little difference to the United States' attitude.

However, Sadat now had strong financial support from the oil-rich state of Saudi Arabia. Also, the new Syrian leader, President Assad, became a close ally. Both Sadat and Assad realised that they would have to act soon if they were to recover Sinai and the Golan Heights, the lands they had lost in 1967. The Israelis were increasing their control of these areas: they were building new Jewish settlements and kept many troops there. Secretly, the Egyptian and Syrian leaders prepared for war.

> **A** In September 1973, in a speech in Cairo, President Sadat said:
>
> **The United States is still under Zionist pressure and is wearing Zionist spectacles. The United States will have to take off those spectacles before they talk to us … We have had enough talk. We know our goal and we are determined to attain it.**

Very few people took Sadat's speech shown in source A seriously. They had heard it all before. So had the Israelis. They had a low opinion of the Arab armies anyway.

The fighting

On 6 October Egypt and Syria attacked. It was **Yom Kippur**, a holiday and the holiest day of the Jewish year. This meant that many soldiers were on leave, Israeli radio was closed down and most of the nation had stopped work. The Israelis were caught

B Egyptians storm across the Suez Canal. At the start of the war, 8000 troops crossed the Canal over ten bridges, by-passing the Israeli strong points. The whole operation had been planned and practised very thoroughly.

completely by surprise. The Egyptians crossed the Suez Canal and took back part of Sinai from the Israelis. At the same time, 500 Syrian tanks overwhelmed Israeli forces on the Golan Heights. The Israeli air force retaliated but discovered that the Arabs had Russian surface-to-air missiles which they used very effectively.

It took the Israeli army three days to become fully **mobilised**. However, by 12 October they had pushed the Syrians back and, on 15 October, they thrust across the Suez Canal and cut off the Egyptian third army (see source A on page 26).

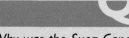

The tank battle which took place on the Golan Heights was the biggest since the Second World War.

(see source A on page 26).

Q

1 Why was the Suez Canal a continuing cause of fighting between Egypt and Israel?
2 Why was Sadat keen to go to war with Israel sooner rather than later?
3 Read source A.
   a) What does Sadat mean when he accuses the United States of wearing 'Zionist spectacles'?
   b) Do you think it is a fair accusation? Give your reasons.
   c) What had he already done to encourage the Americans 'to take off those spectacles'?

THE OIL WAR

Two days after the Israelis crossed the Suez Canal and trapped a whole Egyptian army (see source A), the Arabs produced an unexpected weapon – oil. The West received much of its oil from the Middle East. The Arab oil-producing states decided to reduce oil production until the Israelis withdrew from the lands they had occupied in 1967. The richest oil state, Saudi Arabia, went further. It banned all oil exports to the United States and the Netherlands, the two countries which Saudi Arabia accused of helping the Israelis the most. The West was shocked.

In the 1970s, Europe imported over 85 per cent of its oil from the Arab states.

Both superpowers were keen to be on good terms with each other at this time. American and Russian leaders met and together demanded a cease-fire which the United Nations supported. The fighting ended on 24 October. A few days later UN troops were sent to Egypt to preserve the cease-fire.

The Arabs gain new confidence

The Yom Kippur War was, in the end, a military victory for the Israelis. Yet again they had proved that their weapons, their training and their tactics were superior. But it was a political victory for the Arabs. They had completely surprised the Israelis and the rest of the world with their attack. They had proved that Arab soldiers could fight with courage and determination. Their leaders had shown skill. Above all, they had acted together, especially in the use of the oil weapon. As a result the rest of the world showed much more respect for the Arabs.

One man, in particular, emerged from the war as a hero. Anwar Sadat had achieved exactly what he had set out to do. First, he had broken the stalemate that existed before the war. Secondly, he had forced a change in US policy. The United States was to become far more friendly with the Arab states. A few years later the American government was to play an important part in bringing about peace between Egypt and Israel.

Map key:
- Initial Arab attacks
- Israeli counter attacks

Damascus
SYRIA
Mediterranean Sea
Tel Aviv
Jerusalem
ISRAEL
JORDAN
Suez Canal
The trapped Egyptian army
Cairo
Suez
SINAI
River Nile
Gulf of Suez
EGYPT
SAUDI ARABIA
0 100 200 km
Red Sea

A The Yom Kippur War, 1973.

The superpowers step in

The United States and USSR were deeply involved in the Yom Kippur War. The Russians sent arms to Egypt and Syria and the United States sent them to Israel. When the Israelis crossed the Suez Canal both superpowers stepped in. Russia advised Egypt to accept a cease-fire while it still held part of Sinai. The US government was worried by the Arab oil weapon, as many western countries depended on Arab oil. The United States also hoped to stop its ally, Israel, from attacking Cairo and Damascus for fear that Russian troops might be brought in.

B President Sadat of Egypt. He emerged from the war as a hero.

"Don't worry, Abdul, with this disguise the Americans won't let them shoot!"

C A cartoon from an American newspaper of October 1973, giving a US view of the conflict.

Q

1 Study source C.
  a) Who do Abdul and his friend represent?
  b) Who are the 'them' they refer to?
  c) What is the message of the cartoon?
2 After the Six-Day War of 1967, it seemed as if the Israelis were unbeatable. How do you explain the Arabs' success in 1973?
3 This question is about the causes of all the Arab–Israeli wars from 1948 to 1973. The last part provides an opportunity for extended writing.
  a) Make an enlarged copy of the table shown on the right.
  b) Make notes, on your table, on each of the wars. Then, underline or highlight causes which have been common to more than one war.

The causes of the Arab–Israeli wars from 1948 to 1973	
1948–9	
1956	
1967	
1973	

Extended writing
  c) 'The Arabs' desire to destroy the state of Israel has been the major cause of all the Arab–Israeli wars from 1948 to 1973.' Do you agree with this interpretation? Write 300–500 words to answer this question.
4 How was Israel able to survive four major wars against its Arab neighbours?

A People Without a Home – the Refugee Problem

How serious was the Palestinian refugee problem? What were conditions like in the refugee camps?

Where did the Palestinian refugees go?

During the fighting in 1948–9 between Israel and neighbouring Arab states, about 700 000 Arabs fled from their homes in Palestine. As you can see on the map below, most of them went to the West Bank or the Gaza Strip. Large numbers also went to Syria, Jordan and Lebanon. Today the United Nations reckons there are about 2 500 000 Palestinian refugees.

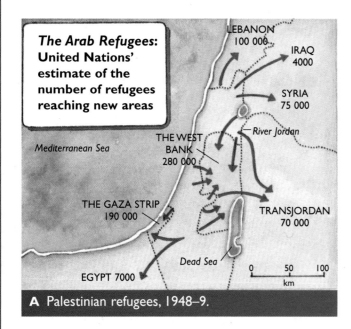

The Arab Refugees: **United Nations' estimate of the number of refugees reaching new areas**

LEBANON 100 000
IRAQ 4000
SYRIA 75 000
River Jordan
Mediterranean Sea
THE WEST BANK 280 000
THE GAZA STRIP 190 000
TRANSJORDAN 70 000
Dead Sea
0   50   100 km
EGYPT 7000

A Palestinian refugees, 1948–9.

The United Nations and the refugees

After the 1948–9 war the United Nations formed the UN Relief and Works Agency (**UNRWA**). This body set up camps for the refugees and provided food, clothing, shelter and education. At first, the refugees lived in tents as in source D. The conditions are described, first by a British observer and then by a refugee himself in sources B and C.

B Jonathan Dimbleby, a British observer, comments in *The Palestinians*:

The conditions in the camps were atrocious. Families huddled bleakly in overcrowded tents. They were without adequate food or sanitation. When it rained, the narrow paths along each row were churned into mud which oozed into the tents. They lived in sodden clothes and slept in wet blankets. Influenza reached epidemic proportions. The young and old perished. Malnourished children were too weak to resist, and the old, left with no purpose, lacked the will.

C Ghazi Daniel, a refugee remembers:

A few months after our arrival, we were penniless and had to move into a refugee camp with 2000 other homeless Palestinians. It is beyond human endurance for a family of eleven to live in a small tent through all the seasons of the year on UNRWA rations. Fathers buried their children who died of hunger. Some buried their fathers who died of disease. On winter days we all crawled together to gain the warmth of humans …

D A refugee camp in Jordan, 1949.

They live in little huts of mud and concrete blocks, corrugated iron roofs, regimented row after row. Fairly adequate medical service is provided, probably better than was enjoyed before they were expelled from their native villages.

Children swarm everywhere. There are primary schools for nearly all of them … There are secondary schools for many of the adolescents. And what will these youths and girls do when they have finished their secondary school training? There is no employment for them in the Strip, and very few can leave it to work elsewhere … the Gaza Strip resembles a vast concentration camp.

They can look to the east and see wide fields, once Arab land, cultivated extensively by a few Israelis, with a chain of kibbutzim guarding the heights or the areas beyond.

What solutions were there to the refugee problem?

The Israelis refused to allow the refugees to return to their lands in Israel. The Israeli 'Law of Return' allows any Jew anywhere in the world to go and live in Israel but forbids Palestinians to do so.

F In 1967, on American television, General Dayan explained:

We want to have a Jewish state. We can absorb the Arabs, but then it won't be the same country … We want a Jewish state like the French have a French state.

The Israelis were very willing to suggest a solution to the refugee problem, as source G shows – follow Israel's example!

G Abba Eban, Israeli ambassador to the United Nations, in a speech in 1958:

There is a similarity of language, religion and background existing between the Arab refugees and their Arab host countries …

Israel with her small territory, her poor water resources and her lack of money, has found homes, work and citizenship in the past ten years for nearly a million newcomers …

If Israel in these conditions could absorb nearly one million refugees – 450 000 of them from Arab lands – how much more easily could the vast Arab world find a home for a similar number of refugees …

But the views of the refugees were very different.

H Ghazi Daniel, who was quoted in source C, had strong views:

I am 24 years old. I was born in Nazareth but today I have no country … The two most precious ideals of my people are to remain Palestinians and not be refugees. These can only be realised if we return to our country and our homes … I am left with no alternative but to fight our enemy.

Not all refugees were inspired to fight for Palestine. Some were offered jobs in their new countries. Some managed to emigrate to other parts of the Middle East or the West. They became engineers, teachers, doctors or businessmen. A small number became very wealthy.

However, most of the refugees remained poor, uneducated and unemployed. Crowded together in the camps, they became frustrated and bitter. It was from the camps that the Palestine Liberation Organisation recruited most of its members.

1 Read sources B and C. What similarities are there in the two accounts of conditions in the camps?
2 Look at source D. To what extent does it support the descriptions in sources B and C?
3 Read source E.
    a) What benefits does the UNRWA bring to the refugees in the camps?
    b) There are other factors, also mentioned in this source, which might turn some of the refugees into fedayeen, or fighters, for the Palestinian cause. What are they?
4 Read source G.
    a) Who are the 'Arab host countries' to which Abba Eban refers? (Look at the map again if you are not sure.)
    b) How many refugees does he say Israel absorbed? Why do you think he mentions '450 000 of them from Arab lands'?
    c) What is his solution to the refugee problem?
5 Read source H.
    a) What reasons would Ghazi Daniel give for opposing Abba Eban's suggestion?
    b) What is his own solution?

The Palestine Liberation Organisation

Why was the Six-Day War a turning point for the Palestine Liberation Organisation? Why did some Palestinians resort to acts of terrorism? What did terrorism achieve?

B One of the hooded Palestinian terrorists on the balcony of the Olympic Village building where the Israeli athletes were held hostage.

The image of the hooded gunman is many people's picture of the terrorist. In the 1970s, this was the image which many people had of the Palestine Liberation Organisation. The man in the photograph (in source B) and eight other Palestinians seized and killed 11 Israeli athletes at the Olympic Games in 1972.

This was not the first time that Arabs or Israelis had carried out what we call terrorist attacks. For example, in 1948, Jewish extremists killed the inhabitants of the Arab village of Deir Yassin (see Chapter 3). In the 1950s and 1960s, Palestinian guerrillas carried out many raids against Israeli villages. But after the Six-Day War, the terrorism spread to Europe and our newspapers reported it in full. In order to understand why this happened we need to study the PLO.

A Two young Fatah members guard the entrance to a military training camp. The guns had live ammunition and no safety catches.

As you learnt in Chapter 6, the PLO was set up in 1964. Its aim was to unite all Palestinians in the struggle to win back their land. The largest group within the PLO was Fatah, which had been set up by Yasser Arafat. From 1965 to 1967, Fatah carried out an increasing number of guerrilla attacks on Israel and was supported by the Arab states which bordered Israel. However, after the Six-Day War of 1967, things were to be very different for the PLO.

Why was the Six-Day War a turning point for the PLO?

Syria, Jordan and Egypt, which had provided vital support for the PLO, were weakened by their heavy losses in the war. At the same time, Egypt and Syria became far more concerned about the lands they had lost to Israel than about the Palestinian refugees. Many Palestinians were now convinced that they would have to fight for their homeland on their own. This was even more urgent now that all the original land of Palestine, including the West Bank and Gaza Strip, was under Israeli rule.

350 000 Palestinians fled from the West Bank when it was captured by the Israelis in the war. Most of the refugees went to Jordan. As a result, Fatah now concentrated its forces in Jordan. Fatah and other groups within the PLO started to recruit far more volunteers in the refugee camps.

> **C** Ghazi Daniel was one of many Palestinian refugees for whom 1967 was a turning point:
>
> The aggressive war of 1967 was a landmark in my life. The new expansion of Israel and the new waves of refugees multiplied the tragedy many times. This is why I have joined the Palestine National Liberation Movement. We shall fight for the Palestinians' return …

Fatah now increased its raids into Israel. In retaliation, in 1968, the Israelis crossed the border into Jordan and launched a full-scale attack on a major Fatah base in Karameh. Although the Israelis destroyed the Palestinian base, the Palestinian forces (with the aid of Jordanian troops) knocked out several Israeli tanks and planes and killed 28 Israeli troops. This inspired thousands of Palestinians to join the Palestinian armed forces. Between 1967 and 1970 Fatah forces killed over 500 Israelis. This was almost as many as the Israelis had lost in the whole Six-Day War.

Arafat becomes leader of the PLO

In 1968 Yasser Arafat became chairman of the PLO. He tried to coordinate the guerrilla activities of the various groups within the organisation. Like most of the PLO leaders, he wanted to limit the raids and the bombings to Israeli territory and Israeli targets because their military aim was strictly war on Israel. However, some **extremist** Palestinian groups caused divisions inside the PLO by making attacks in other parts of the world. They pointed out that raids into Israel had achieved very little. They were impatient. They were not prepared to wait 10 or 20 years to regain their country.

For reasons of security, Yasser Arafat slept in a different bed every night.

D Yasser Arafat was born in Jerusalem in 1929. He was the founder of the Fatah organisation and became chairman of the PLO in 1968.

1 Several reasons are given to explain why the Six-Day War was a turning point for the Palestinians. Select what you think are the three most important reasons and explain your choice.
2 Using your own knowledge and the sources in these last two chapters, explain why many young Palestinians decided to join the PLO armed forces in the late 1960s.
3 What was the main reason for splits developing within the PLO?

HIJACKS AND HOSTAGES

In December 1968 two Palestinians hijacked an Israeli passenger plane at Athens airport, killing one man. The Israelis retaliated by destroying 13 aircraft in an attack on Beirut Airport in Lebanon, which is where the hijackers had come from. In the following years there were many hijackings, kidnappings and bombings in Europe and elsewhere. At first the targets were Israeli planes, embassies and offices, but some targets had very little to do with Israel at all. The Israelis usually responded by bombing Palestinian bases in Lebanon and Syria. Often these bases were near refugee camps so that hundreds of innocent Palestinians died. These Israeli reprisals received far less publicity in the western press than the Palestinian attacks.

Sometimes terrorist violence led Arab to fight Arab. In Jordan, King Hussein feared the Israeli reprisals which followed Palestinian attacks that were launched from his country. In 1968 his troops had helped the Palestinians to inflict heavy casualties on the Israelis at Karameh. However, in September 1970, he decided he did not want any more raids launched on Israel from inside Jordan. Besides, the PLO were acting as if they ruled much of Jordan. So he ordered the Palestinians to obey him and his army.

Then, in the same month, four aircraft were hijacked by Palestinian extremists and three of the planes (belonging to British Airways, Swissair and TWA) were taken to a Palestinian base in Jordan. The passengers were set free but the British plane was blown up (see source A). This made King Hussein fear foreign intervention and he was forced to act. He ordered his army to take control of the PLO bases. The Palestinians resisted and in the next ten days nearly 10 000 of them were killed. The PLO offices in Jordan were shut down and their newspapers banned. The remaining guerrillas went to Syria and Lebanon.

Black September

Palestinian extremists later got their revenge by murdering the Jordanian Prime Minister while he was in Egypt. The killers were members of a group called Black September, named after the month in which the Palestinian bases in Jordan were wiped out. Soon they began sending letter bombs to Israeli embassies in Europe.

Then, on 5 September 1972, they stunned the whole world. They attacked the Israeli athletes who were competing in the Olympic games in Germany. They killed two athletes and then demanded the release of 200 Palestinians in prison in Israel. When German police attempted a rescue, the Palestinians killed nine more athletes. The Palestinians got the massive publicity they wanted for their cause but not the release of their comrades. A few days later the Israelis took their revenge and carried out reprisal raids on Syria and Lebanon, in which over 200 refugees were killed.

B A newspaper headline on the Olympic murders.

A The British plane, which was hijacked by Palestinians, is blown up in Jordan.

The effects on world opinion

Acts of terrorism made the Palestinians unpopular in the rest of the world. People were shocked by such brutal deeds. They branded the PLO, as a whole, as terrorists. However, terrorist acts made many people in Europe and other parts of the world begin to think more about the Palestinian problem. They read about the crowded, unhealthy camps in which hundreds of thousands of refugees had lived for 20 years. They came to understand that the Palestinian people were the helpless victims of war and asked themselves whether the guerrillas were in fact terrorists or freedom fighters.

Terrorists or freedom fighters?

C One Palestinian leader said:

When we hijack a plane it has more effect than if we killed 100 Israelis in battle. For decades world public opinion has been neither for nor against the Palestinians. It simply ignored us. At least the world is talking about us now.

D Sami el-Karami, a Palestinian, said:

The non-violent methods are very beautiful and very easy, and we wish we could win with these methods. Our people do not carry machine guns and bombs because they enjoy killing. It is for us the last resort. For 22 years we have waited for the United Nations and the United States, for liberty, for freedom and democracy. There was no result. So this is our last resort.

E A Palestinian student in Lebanon wrote to his parents in 1968:

For 20 years our people have been waiting for a just solution to the Palestinian problem. All that we got was charity and humiliation while others continue to live in our homes. I refuse to remain a refugee. I have decided to join the freedom fighters and I ask for your blessing.

F A Palestinian woman explained:

I am proud that my son did not die in this refugee camp. The foreign press come here and take pictures of us standing in queues to obtain food rations … This is no life. I am proud that my son died in action, fighting on our occupied soil. I am already preparing my eight-year-old for the day he can fight for freedom too.

In the 1970s it was easy for terrorists to enter planes with guns and grenades. It is only since then that body searches and electronic scans have become routine.

G Hassan, a 17-year-old Palestinian, told a British journalist:

We are not terrorists. We do not bomb women and children. We are against Israel. We are not against the Jews. We want our land back. When a commando goes into Israel he puts a bomb into a place defended by Israelis. The bombs are for the soldiers. If we place a bomb in a bus, it is a bus carrying soldiers, a military target. They are not civilians. If women and children are killed it is by mistake, and we regret it, but we have no alternative.

H This was a typical Israeli point of view in the 1970s:

The PLO is a murderous group of terrorists with more sophisticated weapons than most armies. Israel has no choice but to destroy the PLO's military capability. Israel is fighting a just war!

1 Why did King Hussein order his army to drive the PLO forces out of Jordan?
2 How do sources B and C help to explain why the athletes at Munich were chosen as a terrorist target?
3 a) Use sources D, E and F to explain why some Palestinians have used military force in order to achieve their objectives.
   b) The author of source E writes of 'charity and humiliation'. What evidence of these is there in source F?
   c) Why does the author of source E call himself a 'freedom fighter'? Why does he use this term rather than 'terrorist'?
   d) What is the Israeli view (Source H) of the PLO? How would the Israelis respond to source G?
4 'The views expressed in sources D–H are all biased and therefore of little use to the historian.' Do you agree? Explain your answer in 100–200 words, making reference to all of the sources.

War in Lebanon

Why did the Israelis invade Lebanon in 1978 and 1982? What did they achieve?

Lebanon, 10 April, 1985. A 16-year-old Muslim girl, Sana M'Heidli, set off on a special mission. She drove a car packed with explosives towards a group of Israeli soldiers in Lebanon and then detonated the charge. She killed herself and two Israelis. We know it was a suicide mission because she explained what she was going to do on video beforehand. The photograph below comes from the video. It was later shown on television in Lebanon. What drove her to this desperate act? What were Israeli troops doing in Lebanon anyway?

A Sana M'Heidli, suicide bomber.

Crisis in Lebanon

Until the 1970s Lebanon was a fairly stable country and its capital, Beirut, was one of the richest cities in the Middle East. However, in 1970, the PLO armed forces set up more bases there after they were expelled from Jordan (see page 32). They took over most of the south of Lebanon (some called it 'Fatahland') and frequently bombed villages in northern Israel. The Israelis hit back and, when they did so, Lebanese as well as Palestinians were killed.

In 1975 the Lebanese government ordered its army to regain control of the south. The Palestinians resisted and were helped by Lebanese Muslims. Most of the Lebanese army were Christian and soon there was a civil war between Christians and Muslims.

In 1976, Syrian forces entered Lebanon to end the fighting and restore order. However the PLO continued to carry out attacks on Israel. In 1978 a PLO suicide squad went further south and attacked a bus near Tel Aviv, killing 37 passengers.

Israeli invasions, 1978 and 1982

Three days after the bus bombing, Israeli troops invaded Lebanon. They seized the south of the country but the PLO forces melted away. The Israelis withdrew, under pressure from the United States, and United Nations troops were sent to keep the peace on the Lebanese–Israeli border.

Four years later, in June 1982, a group of Palestinians attempted to murder the Israeli ambassador in London. The Israelis again rolled across the Lebanese border. This time they had 170 000 troops, 3500 tanks and 600 fighter planes. The UN peace-keeping forces were powerless to stop them. The Israelis were more successful in destroying PLO forces than they had been in 1978. However, thousands of Palestinian and Lebanese civilians were killed in the process and hundreds of thousands were made homeless.

The Israelis claimed that their aim was to drive out the Palestinian forces and destroy their bases. However it soon became obvious that this was a full-scale invasion because the Israelis advanced north and surrounded the capital, Beirut. They started shelling positions in the city which were held by the PLO. These positions were often in crowded residential areas so thousands more civilians were killed.

In mid-August, the United States intervened and the Israelis stopped shelling the city. American, French and Italian troops were sent out to supervise the evacuation of PLO guerrillas. Over 14 000 of them left Beirut to travel to other Arab states. Yasser Arafat moved his headquarters to Tunisia.

> On 1 August 1982, Israel began a major attack on Beirut. On that day alone, 127 air raids were carried out over the city.

The Israelis withdraw, 1985

When the PLO forces left Beirut, the Israelis withdrew their troops from the capital but they stayed in the south of Lebanon. The Israelis had succeeded in driving out the Palestinian armed forces but they had made many enemies amongst the Lebanese, especially the Muslims, in the south. Furthermore, they could still not be sure that they had driven out all the Palestinian forces. The guerrillas could easily hide in the huge, crowded refugee camps in Lebanon.

The Israeli government faced further problems. International opinion blamed the Israelis for thousands of civilian deaths. In Israel itself, huge numbers demonstrated against the war. They accused the government of turning a defensive war into an aggressive one and of sending hundreds of Israelis, as well as thousands of Palestinians and Lebanese, to their deaths unnecessarily.

B Israeli opponents of war. Begin was the Prime Minister and Sharon was the Defence Minister in the Israeli government. Raful was the military commander.

Over the next two years, Israeli troops in the south of Lebanon were regularly attacked. When Israelis heard news of events like Sana M'Heidli's attack on their troops, they demanded a complete withdrawal from Lebanon. In 1985, the last Israeli troops finally left Lebanon. This was the longest war Israel had fought. Many regarded it as its first defeat.

Perhaps some good came out of Israel's war in Lebanon. Some Israelis and some Palestinians changed their views.

How did the Lebanon war change Israeli and Palestinian views?

C Jacobo Timerman, an Israeli, wrote in *The Longest War*:

> The Israeli soldiers brought back with them stories about families of up to ten relatives helping each other to survive amid collapse and panic. Stories about children completely different from the rocket-launching children who were the only ones mentioned by official Israeli propaganda. Lost children of ten or twelve caring for their younger brothers … They met Palestinian youths who served as volunteers in hospitals, who have friends, who want to have children some day, and who, like the Israelis, dream of a motorcycle, a girl …

D Later in his book, Timerman wrote about a PLO commander in Lebanon who had decided:

> … that the era of armed struggle was over and that Palestinians should pursue their aims using political, not military, methods. After 18 years of fighting, the PLO commander says 'Another death, whether Israeli or Palestinian, will not solve the problem. On the contrary, it will just make another family unhappy.'

1. Why did some people call South Lebanon 'Fatahland'?
2. In 1978, after the Israeli invasion of Lebanon, 'the PLO forces melted away'. What do you think is meant by this expression? (Clue: many of the PLO forces were based in or near refugee camps.)
3. Sana M'Heidli (source A) said in her pre-recorded video: 'I chose death in order to fulfil my national duty.' What do you think she meant?
4. Look at source B. What is the meaning of the message on the placard? How would you explain it?
5. a) What did Israel achieve by invading Lebanon in 1982?
   b) In what ways did Israel suffer a defeat? (Think of political, as well as military, factors.)
6. a) What is the message of source C?
   b) Why does Timerman refer to 'official Israeli propaganda'?

Peacemaking at the UN and Camp David

What did the PLO achieve by peaceful means? Why did President Sadat go to Israel? What was agreed in the Egypt–Israel peace treaty?

For 30 years, not one of the Arab states was willing to recognise Israel. As far as they were concerned, the state of Israel did not exist. Then, in the 1970s, came a major breakthrough.

After the Yom Kippur War of 1973, Egypt and Syria were still determined to win back the lands they had lost in 1967. But the Egyptians, unlike the Syrians, seemed willing to recognise the state of Israel although they did not admit this in public.

Similarly, Yasser Arafat and some of the PLO leaders sounded more moderate. They hinted that they were ready to consider a 'mini-state' for the Palestinians – consisting of the West Bank and Gaza where the majority of the inhabitants were Palestinian. In other words, the PLO moderates were no longer determined to remove the state of Israel.

The gun and the olive branch – Arafat at the United Nations

The PLO realised the value of foreign political support and set up PLO offices in many countries. PLO officials set out to win the support of foreign governments. At the end of 1974 Yasser Arafat was invited to speak at the United Nations for the first time.

Many of Arafat's listeners at the UN were sympathetic. Some world leaders were beginning to admit that the Palestinians deserved a homeland. They also realised that if the Palestinians could be granted a homeland, then permanent peace in the Middle East was possible.

A Arafat told his audience at the United Nations:

… the roots of the Palestinian question are not the result of a conflict between two religions or two nationalisms. Neither is it a border conflict between two neighbouring states. It is the cause of a people deprived of its homeland, dispersed and uprooted, and living mostly in exile and in refugee camps.

B Yasser Arafat ended his speech to the UN with the words:

Today I have come bearing an olive branch [a symbol of peace] and a freedom fighter's gun. Do not let the olive branch fall from my hand.

Opposition to Arafat

Although Arafat received a sympathetic hearing at the United Nations, he had many enemies elsewhere. The Israelis were furious with the United Nations for inviting Arafat to speak. They said the PLO was a 'murder organisation'. They refused to discuss the idea of a separate Palestinian state, however small it might be. They feared that the Palestinians aimed to take back all of Israel and would not be content with a small state next door to Israel.

The PLO was itself divided. Some extremists still insisted that Israel should be completely destroyed and taken over by Palestinians. They rejected the idea of a Palestinian 'mini-state' and did not want any Arab state to recognise Israel. In the mid-1970s they launched terrorist attacks both inside Israel and in other parts of the world. The Israelis retaliated by bombing the Palestinian bases and refugee camps in Lebanon.

Sadat flies to Israel, 1977

After the Yom Kippur War in 1973, the United States government worked hard to bring peace to the Middle East. The Americans persuaded the Israelis and the Egyptians to draw back their forces on the Suez Canal in January 1974. In March, Saudi Arabia started selling oil to the United States again. In May, Syria and Israel agreed to separate their forces on the Golan Heights. The following year the Suez Canal was reopened and the Israeli and Egyptian forces drew back on the Sinai front also. A United Nations force kept the two sides apart.

The bravest peacemaker was undoubtedly President Sadat of Egypt. He wanted permanent peace for his own country. Four wars against Israel had cost many lives and much money. Egypt needed a lasting peace in order to recover. In 1977 he surprised the world by announcing that he was willing to go to Israel and discuss peace. This was a bold move: for 30 years Arab leaders had refused even to accept Israel's existence. Ten days later he flew to Israel.

The following month the Israeli Prime Minister, Menachem Begin, went to Egypt and peace talks were started. When they slowed down in 1978, US President Carter invited the Egyptian and Israeli leaders to Camp David in the United States. For 13 days the three men and their advisers discussed a peace settlement.

The Camp David agreements of 1978

The whole Middle East conflict was discussed at Camp David but the most important agreement reached was the one which paved the way for a peace treaty between Israel and Egypt. Source D is an outline of the agreement.

D The framework for an Egypt–Israel peace treaty:

- Egypt to regain all of Sinai within three years.
- Israeli forces to be withdrawn from Sinai.
- Israeli shipping will have free passage through the Suez Canal and the Straits of Tiran (see map on page 22).

E Sadat, Carter and Begin shake hands after reaching a peace agreement in September 1978.

The Egypt–Israel peace treaty, March 1979

Six months after Camp David, the Egyptian and Israeli leaders signed a peace treaty. The Israelis agreed to withdraw from Sinai and the Egyptians agreed to allow Israeli ships to pass through the Suez Canal and the Straits of Tiran. Both sides finally agreed to recognise 'each other's right to live in peace within their secure and recognised boundaries'.

Arab opposition to Sadat

There was opposition to Sadat throughout the Arab world. Many accused him of breaking Arab unity by making peace with Israel. They said he had betrayed the Arab cause and several Arab states stopped all trade with Egypt.

Despite the opposition in the Arab world, the signing of the Egypt–Israel peace treaty was a great breakthrough in Arab–Israeli relations. However, the Palestinian problem still remained at the heart of the conflict in the Middle East. A solution seemed as far off as ever.

'The time of the flight from Cairo to Jerusalem is short but the distance until last night was almost infinite.' Israeli Prime Minister to President Sadat, 20 November 1977.

Q

1 In the Egypt–Israel peace treaty, land was traded for security.
   a) Who gained the land?
   b) Who gained the security?
2 Read source B. What do you think Arafat meant?
3 Why do you think Yasser Arafat was invited to speak at the United Nations? Here are three possible reasons:
   a) The PLO was beginning to sound more moderate and more peaceful.
   b) The Yom Kippur War (see Chapter 7, page 26) had made governments in the West more sympathetic to the Arabs.
   c) Palestinian terrorism had forced the rest of the world to take more notice of the Palestinian problem.
   How might each of these explain the invitation? Which do you think was most important?

The Role of the Superpowers (the United States and the USSR)

A A cartoon from the British magazine *Punch*, November 1967. The two figures in the cartoon represent Johnson and Brezhnev, the American and Russian leaders.

The cartoon above shows the United States and the USSR pouring arms into the 'boiling pot' of the Middle East. This chapter will examine how and why the two superpowers became involved in the conflict.

The United States, with its large and influential Jewish population, played a major part in the creation of the Jewish state of Israel (as you saw in Chapter 3). The USSR also supported the new state at that time because it believed that the Jews needed a state of their own.

Then, in the 1950s, the USSR responded to Egypt's request for weapons. With the **Cold War** between the United States and the USSR

developing, Soviet Russia saw a great opportunity to win allies, and to balance America's influence, in the Middle East.

The superpowers and the Suez War, 1956

In the Suez War of 1956, both the USSR and the United States condemned Anglo-French military action against Egypt (see Chapter 5). However, it was the Russians who gained most.

B In 1981, British historians Bown and Mooney wrote:

> The Suez war was a bonus for the Soviet Union and a disaster for the West. It seriously damaged Anglo-French and western prestige in the Middle East. Egypt and Syria turned increasingly to the Soviet Union for the arms and aid that they needed. Suez gave the USSR a foothold in the Middle East.

After the 1956 war, the USSR increased its support, both with weapons and military advisers, to the leading Arab states. Similarly, the United States continued to arm Israel. In fact, the United States gave billions of dollars of financial aid and weapons to Israel (and still does today). The United States felt that Israel was its only close, firm friend in the Middle East. And, of course, America's Jewish population put a lot of pressure on its government to support Israel (which, again, it also still does today).

The Six-Day War, 1967

As you learnt in Chapter 6, the Six-Day War was an overwhelming victory for the Israelis. Israel's Arab opponents, especially Egypt and Syria, were devastated. However, the Soviet Union immediately began to re-equip Egypt and Syria, while the United States provided more weapons for Israel's armed forces.

The Yom Kippur War, 1973

In the Yom Kippur War of 1973, both the superpowers poured arms into the conflict in order to support their allies.

Big Two send arms

THE MIDDLE EAST conflict took on a new dimension of danger last night as both Russia and America began airlifting fresh weapons to each side.

C On 11 October 1973, the *Daily Mail* reported:

The superpowers also played a big part in ending the war. Both sides wanted to avoid being dragged into the fighting and had their own reasons for wanting to ease the tension in the Cold War. (You can read how the superpowers brought about a cease-fire on page 26.)

D A blindfolded Russian military adviser is led away by Israeli troops during the Israeli advance into Syria in 1967.

The Arab use of the 'oil weapon' in the Yom Kippur War shocked the Americans and, over the next few years, the United States government did much to improve its relations with the Arab world and to bring peace to the region. In 1978, the US President, Jimmy Carter, brought the Israeli and Egyptian leaders together at Camp David and, a year later, the Egypt–Israel peace treaty was signed (see page 37). The United States now began to supply both money and weapons to Egypt.

The end of the Cold War

Towards the end of the 1980s, relations between the United States and the USSR improved. As the communist system of government crumbled and the Soviet Union broke up, Russian influence in the Middle East faded. Countries like Syria could no longer rely on Russian arms and financial support. This meant that the United States no longer had to support Israel in order to maintain its influence in the Middle East.

In 1991 the United States, now the only remaining superpower, formed a multi-national military force to drive Iraqi troops out of Kuwait (see page 42). Even Russia and its former ally, Syria, supported the Americans. Later in the same year, the United States government put pressure on the Israelis (by holding back money and weapons) in order to get them to hold peace talks with the Palestinians. Two years later Israel and the PLO signed a peace agreement. You will read more about this in Chapter 14.

> Between 1948 and 1997, the United States gave Israel $85 billion in aid.

E In 1994, a British journal stated:

In finding a peaceful solution to the Palestinian problem, much will depend on the US government, Israel's main financial backer and friend. American aid to Israel is more than $3 billion a year. This gives the US considerable leverage [influence] in the politics of peacemaking.

1 What reasons can you suggest for the United States' support for Israel?
2 What evidence of superpower involvement in the Arab–Israeli conflict is there in sources C and D?
3 Read source E. Explain what is meant by the United States' 'leverage [influence] in the politics of peacemaking'.

Extended writing

Source B states: 'The Suez War was a bonus for the Soviet Union [Russia] and a disaster for the West [United States, Britain and France].' How far do you agree with this interpretation of the Suez War? (You will need to look again at Chapter 5, page 17, as well as this chapter, in order to answer this question.)

The Intifada

Why did a Palestinian uprising break out in the occupied territories in 1987? What effects did it have on Palestinians and Israelis?

On 8 December 1987, an Israeli army vehicle in Gaza crashed into a lorry, killing four of the Palestinians on board. Rumours spread, that it had been a deliberate act of revenge for the killing of an Israeli two days before. The funerals of the Palestinians became huge demonstrations. At one of them a youth was shot dead by an Israeli soldier. As tension mounted, thousands of Palestinians took to the streets, both in Gaza and on the West Bank, and put up barricades of tyres, corrugated iron and building materials. From behind them, they stoned Israeli army patrols.

What was life like for Palestinians living under Israeli military rule in Gaza and the West Bank? Why did these conditions lead to the **Intifada** or 'uprising'?

Life in the occupied territories

Thousands of Israeli troops were stationed in Gaza and the West Bank. They rounded up PLO suspects and others who they saw as a threat to their security. Many were either jailed or deported (usually to Jordan). Sometimes their houses were blown up, leaving their families homeless.

The Israeli army also confiscated land for the building of Jewish settlements. These were built for security reasons, to keep an eye on the Palestinians. It was not only houses that were built.

A In 1979 an Israeli minister said:

Not only should there be settlements: there should be roads which will link the towns and settlements. And not only roads: there should be army camps and military training areas.

On the West Bank, however, there was another reason: for many Israelis, this area is known as Judea and Samaria, part of the ancient land of Israel, the land that God had promised for the Israelites.

B Young Palestinians hurl stones at Israeli soldiers in Gaza.

It became a common sight for the Palestinians to see Jewish settlements being built on land they considered to be theirs.

By 1987, there were over 80 000 Jews living in settlements in and around Jerusalem and another 20 000 living in parts of the West Bank and in Gaza. The Intifada may have been triggered by a single incident but years of living under Israeli occupation had led to increasing hatred and tension.

The Israeli response to the Intifada

The Intifada took everyone by surprise – Israel, the PLO, the Arab states and the rest of the world. Not surprisingly, the Israeli government insisted on an 'iron fist' policy. Live ammunition was used. Newspapers and television around the world showed teenagers being shot by Israeli troops. This led the Israeli government to announce that it would no longer use bullets. Instead, a policy of 'might, power and beatings' would be adopted. But still the death toll rose and worldwide publicity was given to the tear-gassing of demonstrators, the beatings of youths, the closing of schools and colleges. By September 1988, 346 Palestinians had been killed. Many of them were under 16.

Voices of the Intifada – Palestinians and Israelis speak out

Almost every Palestinian family living in the occupied territories was affected by the Intifada. So were many Israeli families because thousands of soldiers, whether regular troops or reservists, were called up to do military service on the West Bank or in Gaza. The following extracts were all taken from interviews conducted in the years after the Intifada began.

By 1991, over 1000 Palestinians had been killed in the Intifada, over 2000 homes destroyed and 15 000 people imprisoned.

C Ali, aged 23, who lives in a refugee camp on the West Bank:

Before the Intifada began, we, the Palestinian people, were already convinced of the justice of our struggle. For the rest of the world, other problems were more pressing. But because of the Intifada, the entire world has now been able to see what is happening in this land. Now some nations see the nature of the Occupation here and see the Palestinian people demanding their rights, demanding a state.

D Amnon, an Israeli on military service in Gaza:

I didn't understand why they hate me. I spoke to one Palestinian girl. I told her I don't hate her. She said she hates us. She sees us all as Nazis. Someone tried to kill me. He stood above me with a rock. He was on the roof and I pointed my gun at him and told him in Arabic that I would shoot him. He said 'Shoot me, I don't care.' He aimed and threw the rock at me. I jumped to one side, escaping the stone.

E Umm Assad, a Palestinian woman who lives in a refugee camp in Gaza:

At one o'clock in the morning the soldiers came into my house. They asked if there were any men here, and I said yes. They took one son who was studying at the university. They said he was doing bad things. They demanded a fine. We gave them the money but he was still tried and imprisoned. Then they came again and took another son who had been wounded. He was sleeping in his bed. Again they came in the middle of the night, not during the day. The boy wanted to go to university, to go abroad to study, and instead they came and took him. He has been in prison for fifteen months. We are not well off, yet we paid their fines; life has to go on. But meanwhile they continue to arrest the youth, to kill them in the streets.

F Alon, an Israeli on military service on the West Bank:

The soldiers caught a child. The commander arrived, he grabbed the child and told him: 'Climb up on the electrical pole' – it was a high-tension wire – 'and take down the PLO flag.' It was a huge pole, impossible to climb. He started and after a few meters he could not go on. The commander started to hit the child in the legs and told him to go on climbing. I was in shock but the soldiers were enjoying it. Then the father came out of the house and he started to cry: 'Leave my child alone, I'll take it down.' He started climbing. He was quite old and couldn't do it. Then he said: 'Wait a minute. I'll bring ladders.' But he still couldn't get to the flag. And the commander started hitting him. I started crying. I started to fight with the commander. He said: 'They put it there. They can take it down.' I asked: 'How will he get it down? It's impossible.' We were actually fighting in front of the soldiers, and finally he gave in. They did not bring down the flag.

1 Why do you think so many Jewish settlements were built in and near Jerusalem?

2 'The continued building of new Israeli settlements in the occupied territories led to the outbreak of the Intifada.' Do you agree with this interpretation?

3 What was the Israeli government's response to the Intifada?

4 a) What does Ali (source C) think was the main achievement of the Intifada?
   b) What does he mean by 'the Occupation'?

5 Read source D again. Why do you think Amnon did not shoot the person with the rock?

6 a) What effects did the Intifada have on the soldiers quoted in sources D and F? How would you explain these effects?
   b) Why would this increase the difficulties which the Israelis had in crushing the Intifada?

7 'Sources C, D, E and F represent the views of ordinary people, not political leaders. Therefore they are more reliable as evidence for the historian studying the effects of the Intifada.' Do you agree with this statement? Write 100–200 words to answer this question.

The Israeli–Palestinian Peace Agreement, 1993

Key Issues > **What finally brought Israeli and Palestinian leaders together? What was agreed in 1993? How far has peace been achieved?**

At the height of the Intifada, in December 1988, the United States opened secret talks with PLO officials. The Americans persuaded Yasser Arafat to do something he had never done before: publicly, he rejected terrorism. Now, at last, the United States was willing to negotiate openly with the PLO and to put more pressure on the Israelis to open peace talks with the Palestinians.

The Iraqi invasion of Kuwait, 1990

Before any peace talks between Israel and the Palestinians were started, another conflict in the Middle East grabbed the headlines. In August 1990, Iraqi troops invaded Kuwait, another Arab state. The Iraqis claimed that Kuwait belonged to them. Most of the Arab world, as well as other countries, condemned the Iraqi attack. The United States rushed troops to the Middle East. The United Nations called for Iraq to withdraw and the Americans led a huge multi-national force which, by the end of February 1991, had driven the Iraqis out of Kuwait.

Palestinians and other Arabs were quick to point out what they saw as the United States' double standards. They said that the Americans had acted swiftly to enforce the UN demand for Iraq to withdraw from Kuwait yet they had not managed, even after 20 years, to persuade Israel to withdraw its troops from the occupied territories of Gaza and the West Bank. The UN had demanded this as far back as 1967 (see page 21).

The US government was stung by this criticism. It wanted to keep the support of Arab states like Egypt, Saudi Arabia, even Syria, who had joined the United States in the fight against Iraq. Also, America's allies in the West depended on imports of oil from Arab states. So the US government was at last willing to put more pressure on Israel. It was now in a better position to do so.

The reason for this change was that the Cold War (between the United States and Soviet Russia) had now ended. The communist government in Russia was, by this time, collapsing. It was no longer supporting the Arab states so strongly. This meant that the United States did not have to support Israel in order to contain a Russian threat in the Middle East any longer. The US government could therefore push the Israelis into making peace. It threatened to hold back money and arms from Israel. In fact, the United States could actually cooperate with Russia because Russia was now desperate for US financial aid. This meant that the United States could also expect the cooperation of Arab leaders who would no longer be able to rely on Russia for arms and money.

The Madrid Conference, 1991

In October 1991, the US government persuaded the Israelis to hold face-to-face talks with Palestinian leaders. By now, an increasing number of both Israelis and Palestinians were coming to the conclusion that they had more to gain from making peace than making war. These talks were held in Madrid. Little progress was made in the talks while the extremists on both sides attempted to disrupt the discussions by acts of violence.

The breakthrough, September 1993

In 1993, discussions were started up again. This time they were held in secret, in neutral Norway, away from the glare of worldwide publicity. In June 1993, the Israeli people elected a new government, which promised to work for peace with the Palestinians. Finally, in September, after eight months of secret talks, the PLO leader, Yasser Arafat, and the head of the new Israeli government, Yitzhak Rabin, exchanged letters.

Arafat, in his letter, rejected the use of terrorism, called for an end to the Intifada and recognised 'the right of Israel to exist in peace and security'. He had never made such clear statements before. Rabin, in his letter, recognised 'the PLO as the representative of the Palestinian people'. In the past, the Israeli government had refused to believe that the PLO really represented the Palestinian people and had regarded the PLO as just a terrorist organisation.

The 1993 peace agreement

On 13 September 1993, the two leaders signed an agreement. This paved the way for a step-by-step approach towards self-government for the Palestinians. Then, in front of all the world's cameras at the White House in Washington, Arafat and Rabin shook hands. It would have been almost impossible to imagine this happening a few years before. At last, a major breakthrough had been made in resolving the Palestinian problem, the problem of a people without a land.

A Rabin and Arafat shake hands. Millions of Israelis and Palestinians celebrated the peace agreement. But not all were happy. Violence erupted amongst Palestinians in many parts of the Middle East. Two years later, Yitzhak Rabin was assassinated by a fellow Israeli, a Jewish religious extremist, who opposed any agreement with the Palestinians.

B The *Daily Mail* wrote:

HANDSHAKE FOR HISTORY

This was the moment no one had dared hope for, organised for a worldwide TV audience by President Clinton on the South Lawn of the White House. At Clinton's right hand was Israeli Prime Minister Yitzhak Rabin, a former general in the Six-Day War when Israel grabbed the occupied territories, including Gaza and the West Bank, from the Arabs. To his left was Yasser Arafat, mastermind of a long terrorist war against Israel. Once bitter enemies, they were risking their political lives on an agreement giving Palestinians self-rule in the Gaza Strip and part of the West Bank in return for official recognition of the Jewish state.

What was agreed?

The Israeli and Palestinian leaders agreed that:

- Israeli troops would be withdrawn from Gaza and the city of Jericho on the West Bank. After that, they would be withdrawn from other parts, but not all, of the West Bank.
- Elections would be held for a Palestinian Council (or Authority) to run the West Bank and Gaza for five years.
- During these five years a final settlement would be discussed.

Within a year, Israeli troops were withdrawn from Gaza and Jericho, as agreed. Elections were held for a Palestinian Council and the PLO won the majority of the seats. By 1997, Israeli troops had withdrawn from most of the West Bank.

> Polls carried out on the West Bank and in Gaza showed that two-thirds of the Palestinian population supported the peace agreement.

C July 1994. PLO leader Yasser Arafat waves to Palestinians on his way into Gaza. It was the first time he had set foot on Palestinian land for 27 years.

1 Why were some Palestinians and other Arabs angry about the United States' role against Iraq?
2 How did the end of communism in Russia help to bring about moves towards peace?
3 'By the early 1990s, an increasing number of Israelis and Palestinians wanted to make peace.' How far do you think the Intifada would explain this?

15

The Problems of Peacemaking

Key Issue **What was to be discussed and decided before a final settlement could be agreed?**

The peace agreement was intended to build confidence and trust between the Israelis and the Palestinians. This it did. The most difficult questions were to be discussed over the next five years before a final settlement could be agreed. These were the main issues:

1 *The future of Jerusalem.* Both Israelis and Palestinians wanted it as their capital. The Israelis were determined to ensure that they continued to control all of the city and that it remained their capital. By the late 1990s East Jerusalem, which was mostly Arab, was encircled by Israeli settlements containing 150 000 Israelis.

2 *The Palestinian refugees' right to return.* Would the refugees in Lebanon, Syria, Jordan and other Arab countries be allowed to return to the homes they had left during the fighting in 1948–9? Most Israelis believed that the Palestinians should not be allowed to return. The Israelis were not willing to turn Jewish Israelis out of the houses they had lived in, and off the land they had farmed, for many years. Most important of all, in the eyes of the Israelis, the Jews would be swamped if all the Palestinian refugees returned and the Palestinians might then form the majority of the population of Israel!

3 *Jewish settlements in the occupied territories.* What would happen to the numerous Israeli settlements on the West Bank ? Should they be given up? If not, should Israeli troops continue to guard those settlements and protect the Jewish inhabitants?

4 *An independent Palestinian state.* Would most Palestinians agree to a state which was limited to the West Bank and Gaza or would many demand *all* of Palestine (meaning the end of Israel)? Even if a Palestinian state was limited to the West Bank and Gaza, Palestinians would surely want a completely independent state. Yet if Israeli troops stayed on the West Bank, then it would not be part of a completely independent Palestine, simply because Jewish (i.e. foreign) troops were stationed there. The Israelis, for their part, were worried about their security as the map (source G) shows. They suspected that many Palestinians would not be satisfied with a mini-state and that Israel would constantly face the threat of destruction.

Attitudes to the 'peace process'

A Faisal Husseini, a Palestinian writer and spokesman for the West Bank Palestinians:

We have decided to get rid of some of our grand dreams. Instead of having our state in all our homeland, we are realistic in deciding to accept a state in only part of our homeland, alongside the state of Israel.

B David Hammo, an Israeli, who was born in Morocco and came to Israel as a boy:

Eventually there will be a Palestinian state, and this has penetrated the dreams of every Israeli. Everyone knows it is inevitable, it is just a question of time.

C A Palestinian refugee in Lebanon said:

I have 16 children, six of whom died as martyrs. My house was destroyed by the Israelis. We have made all these sacrifices and for what? For only Gaza and the West Bank? No, it's not big enough. Where is my home in Acre [in Israel]? We made sacrifices for the whole of Palestine, not for a small part.

D Benny Katzover, an Israeli who lives in a Jewish settlement on the West Bank:

A Palestinian state will never be established. It cannot be established. No government in Israel, or anywhere else, can simply remove the 140 000 Jews who live in Judea and Samaria [the West Bank], the 160 000 Jews in East Jerusalem, or the 150 Jewish settlements.

In the late 1980s and early 1990s, over half a million Jews from the old Soviet Union emigrated to Israel. These arrivals increased the population of Israel by more than 10 per cent. Many of these new immigrants settled on the West Bank.

E 'No going home?' A Palestinian refugee in Lebanon. In 1997, an Arab information service in Britain wrote: 'Keeping millions of Palestinians without a homeland will amount to leaving an unexploded bomb under any peace agreement signed.'

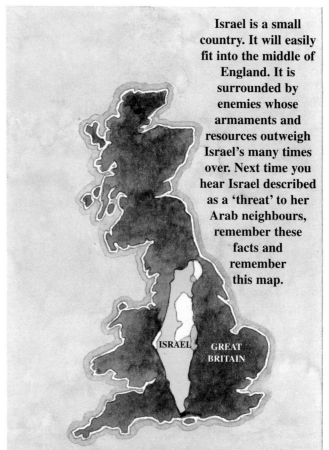

Israel is a small country. It will easily fit into the middle of England. It is surrounded by enemies whose armaments and resources outweigh Israel's many times over. Next time you hear Israel described as a 'threat' to her Arab neighbours, remember these facts and remember this map.

ISRAEL   GREAT BRITAIN

G The map that speaks louder than words. This is adapted from a pamphlet produced by The Britain/Israel Public Affairs Centre.

F Jewish settlers carry out their own patrols on the West Bank and are heavily armed. After the peace agreement of 1993, the building of new settlements, and of more roads to link them, continued.

Q

1 Read sources A, B, C and D. Which of these authors do you think would be willing to accept a Palestinian state consisting of the West Bank and Gaza?
2 Why would the authors of sources C and D oppose the 1993 peace agreement?
3 Source G highlights Israelis' fears about their nation's security. How does it do this?

Extended writing
'There can be no permanent peace unless agreement can be reached on Jewish settlements, the status of Jerusalem and refugees.' Do you agree with this interpretation? Are there other major obstacles to peace? Using the sources, and all you have learnt about the Palestinian problem in this book, write 200–400 words to explain whether you agree with this interpretation.

Prospects for Peace

Since the 1993 agreement much progress has been made in peacekeeping in the Middle East. In 1994, Jordan signed a treaty with Israel in which the two sides settled their dispute over their borders. More importantly, Jordan became the second Arab state (after Egypt in 1978) to recognise the state of Israel and to open up trade and other links. Talks have also been held between Israel and its most bitter enemy, Syria.

But the heart of the Middle East conflict remains the Palestinian problem. The real test of peacemaking will be the success which both Israeli and Palestinian leaders have in controlling their extremists and keeping the support of the majority of their people. On both sides there will always be extremists and those who want to destroy any compromise. On the Israeli side are those who believe that the West Bank must remain in Israeli hands because it is the 'promised land' that God gave to the Jews. On the Palestinian side are those who still believe that all of Palestine must be restored to the Palestinians, even if it means the destruction of Israel.

B Bulldozing the peace process, 1997. Miryam al-Banna, a Palestinian, grieves over the loss of her Jerusalem home, knocked down by the Israelis.

An official Israeli view

After the 1997 bombing (see source A), the Israeli Prime Minister said: 'We expect the Palestinian Authority [Council] and its leader, Arafat, to begin to fight terror, to take all the steps required against these terrorists who roam free.' What steps might the Palestinian Council be expected to take?

An official Palestinian view

In 1997, Afif Safieh, the PLO representative in London, said: 'The continued building of new Jewish settlements on the West Bank and near Jerusalem is a war against the Palestinians, not part of any peace process.' What did he mean?

Despite the bombing and the bulldozing, millions of Israelis and Palestinians want peace. Yet even after 50 years of war, a lasting peace still seems a long way off.

A Bombing the peace process. Israelis lift a dead body onto a stretcher. On 30 July 1997 two men, dressed in suits and carrying briefcases, walked into the market in Jerusalem and pulled the cords on their twin bombs. They killed themselves and 12 others. Hamas, an extremist Palestinian group, said that it was responsible for the attack. Their aim: to destroy the peace talks and the state of Israel.

In 1996, a Palestinian police officer on the West Bank was asked what it was like working alongside Israeli troops (i.e. recent enemies). He said: 'Peace is made between enemies, not between friends.'

Glossary

anti-Semitism – actions or feelings of hatred against the Jews

blockade – the blocking of a place by troops or ships to prevent goods reaching it

Cold War – the state of tension (but not actual war) which existed between the Soviet Union and the USA from the late 1940s to the late 1980s

extremist – a person who has very strong opinions or aims which he or she refuses to change in any circumstances

Fatah – a Palestinian organisation which carried out raids against Israel

fedayeen – men trained to carry out raids (literally, those who sacrifice themselves)

guerrilla – a soldier who avoids fighting in open battle when possible; he prefers to use tactics like ambushes and hit-and-run raids

Haganah – a Jewish defence force set up in the 1920s

Holocaust – the mass murder of the Jews in the Second World War

immigration – the arrival of people to settle in a new country

Intifada – the Palestinian uprising in the West Bank and Gaza in the 1980s

Irgun – a small, secret Jewish organisation which fought for Jewish independence

mandate – power given to a country to look after another country

mobilise – getting an army ready to fight

nationalise – the government taking over ownership of a company, industry or land

occupied territories – lands controlled by the troops of a foreign power (e.g. the West Bank and Gaza, occupied by the Israelis)

partition – division into two or more parts

persecute – to punish or treat cruelly, often because of religion or race

PLO – Palestine Liberation Organisation

propaganda – persuading people to believe certain ideas and behave in a certain way; sometimes involves telling lies

provenance – where a source comes from. Who wrote it? When? Who was intended to read it? What role did the writer have? Provenance is important when deciding the reliability of a source

refugees – people forced to leave their home by war or natural disaster

reprisal – an action against an enemy to stop him from doing something again

settlement – a group of houses (e.g. as built by the Israelis on the West Bank and in Gaza)

synagogue – a building where Jews worship

UNRWA – United Nations Relief and Works Agency, which was set up to run the refugee camps

Yom Kippur – (Day of Atonement) an important Jewish religious day of fasting and annual Jewish holiday

Zionist – someone who believed that the Jews should have a national homeland and, later, an independent state

Index

Aqaba 17–19, 23
Arafat, Yasser 31, 34, 36–7, 42–3, 46
Assad, President 24
Balfour Declaration 3
Begin, Menachem 10–11, 35, 37
Ben-Gurion, David 12, 15
Camp David 36–37, 39
Carter, President 37, 39
Clinton, President 43
Dayan, General 17, 21, 29
Deir Yassin 10–11, 30
Eden, Anthony 15
Eilat 17
Fatah 18, 30–31, 34
fedayeen 13, 17

Gaza 13–15, 20, 22–23, 28–29, 36, 40–45
Golan Heights 20, 22–25, 36
Haganah 7, 10
Holocaust 8, 10
Hussein, King 19, 32–33
Intifada 40–43
Irgun 8, 10–11
Jerusalem 6, 10–12, 20–22, 26, 37, 40, 44, 46
King David Hotel 8–10
Mandates 4–5, 14
Nasser, President 14–19, 24
Palestine Liberation Organisation (PLO) 18, 29–37, 39–40, 42–43, 46

Partition 7, 10–11
Rabin, Yitzhak 42–43
Sadat, President 24–26, 36–37
Sharm-el-Sheikh 17
Sinai 16–17, 20–26
Six-Day War 18–24, 30–31, 38
Suez Canal 14–17, 24–26, 36–39
Tiran, Straits of 15, 17, 19, 37
United Nations Organisation (UN) 9–12, 14, 16, 18–21, 26, 28–29, 34, 36–37, 42
West Bank 13, 20, 22–23, 26, 28, 31, 36, 40–46
Yom Kippur War 24–27, 36–39
Zionists 3, 12

Acknowledgements

The front cover shows Rabin and Arafat with President Clinton outside the White House, reproduced courtesy of Sygma.

The Publishers would like to thank the following for permission to reproduce material in this volume:

Britain/Israel Public Affairs Centre (BIPAC) for an extract from 'Getting it straight: Israel in Perspective' and for the material which was adapted and used in the artwork on page 45; Cassell for an extract from *Full Circle* by A Eden (1960); Croom Helm for an extract from *The Elusive Peace* by W Polk (1979); Friendship Press for extracts from *Justice and the Intifada* by K Bergen *et al.* (1991); Heinemann for an extract from *Cold War to Détente, 1945–80* by Bown and Mooney (1981); Picador for an extract from *The Longest War* by J Timerman (1982); the extract taken from *The Palestinians* by J Dimbleby published by Quartet Books in 1979; Routledge for extracts from *Reporting the Arab–Israeli Conflict* by T Liebes (1997) and *The Question of Palestine* by E Said (1980); European School Books Publishing Ltd for extracts from *Understanding Global Issues* a series of pamphlets edited by Richard Buckley (1994); The Daily Mail for extracts from *The Daily Mail* from 11 November 1973 and 1993; The Spectator for an extract from *The Spectator* 12 May 1961; Weidenfeld and Nicolson for an extract from *Story of my Life* by M Dayan (1976); Steimatzky Ltd for an extract from *The Revolt* by Menachem Begin (1951).

The Publishers would like to thank the following for permission to reproduce the following copyright illustrations in this volume:

Associated Press pp21l, 25, 31, 35, 43r, 46b; Corbis pp6, 12a, 14, 18, 28, 30b, 32b, 37, 40; Hulton Getty pp3, 39b; Israel Defence Force p20; John Frost Historical Newspaper Library pp2l, 8r, 15, 32a, 39a; Network Photography p60; Courtesy of Rob Lawlor, Philadelphia p27; Popperfoto pp7, 8l, 9, 10a and b, 12b, 16, 21r, 30a; Private Collection p19; Punch p38; Sipa Press pp34, 35; Sygma p43l; TRH Pictures pp5, 25.

(**a** above; **b** below; **r** right; **l** left)

Every effort has been made to trace and acknowledge ownership of copyright. The Publishers will be glad to make suitable arrangements with any copyright holders whom it has not been possible to contact.

In memory of John Aylett, who devised this series, and to my children Lizzie and James.

Order queries: please contact Bookpoint Ltd, 39 Milton Park, Abingdon, Oxon OX14 4TD. Telephone: (44) 01235 400414, Fax: (44) 01235 400454. Lines are open from 9.00 - 6.00, Monday to Saturday, with a 24 hour message answering service. Email address: orders@bookpoint.co.uk

British Library Cataloguing in Publication Data
A catalogue record for this title is available from The British Library

ISBN 0 340 71127 4

First published 1998
Impression number 10, 9, 8, 7, 6, 5, 4, 3, 2, 1
Year   2002, 2001, 2000, 1999, 1998

Copyright © 1998 Michael Scott-Baumann

All rights reserved. No part of this publication may be reproduced or transmitted in any form or by any means, electronic or mechanical, including photocopy, recording, or any information storage and retrieval system, without permission in writing from the publisher or under licence from the Copyright Licensing Agency Limited. Further details of such licences (for reprographic reproduction) may be obtained from the Copyright Licensing Agency Limited, of 90 Tottenham Court Road, London W1P 9HE.

Typeset by GreenGate Publishing Services, Tonbridge, Kent.
Printed in Spain for Hodder & Stoughton Educational, a division of Hodder Headline Plc, 338 Euston Road, London NW1 3BH by Mateu Chromo.